WELCOME TO
Live Yourself Happy

ACHIEVE TRUE HAPPINESS AND FEEL MORE FULFILLED

Happiness means different things to different people – what makes one person happy might make another feel unhappy, and vice versa. However, science has shown that there are some fundamental things we can all do to ensure we start living our happiest lives. The decisions we make, our behaviour and, most importantly, our mindset all contribute towards this end goal. Gaining a greater understanding of ourselves will help us to make the right choices so we can avoid negativity, be more authentic, and start living more content and fulfilled lives.

Why do we feel certain emotions in specific situations? Why do we behave in particular ways? And what can we do to overcome the things that hold us back? Learn all this and more by delving into the world of psychology to build a better relationship with your mind. Packed full of expert guidance from psychologists, counsellors and other professionals, in the pages that follow, we look at how to build better relationships, the benefits of having fun, and why decluttering can be great for our wellbeing. We also look into ways to stress better, how to forgive, the thrill of anticipation and more.

The mind is a powerful tool. Learn how to take control of your own mind today for a happier tomorrow.

Contents

6 YOUR MENTAL HEALTH MASTERCLASS

12 WHICH THERAPY IS FOR ME?

16 HOW TO STRESS BETTER

18 PANICKED? PRESS PAUSE

22 MAKE ME-TIME A MUST-DO

25 FIND YOUR MANTRA

26 WHY WE SHOULD ALL BE MORE SELFISH

28 THE GIFT OF COMPASSION

29 WHY IT'S GOOD TO CRY

30 REDISCOVER YOUR OPTIMISM

34 SURVIVAL OF THE KINDEST

38 GRATITUDE AND WELLBEING

42 ACHIEVING FORGIVENESS

44 LEARNING TO TRUST

46 REGRETS ARE GOOD FOR YOU

48 YOU CAN'T CONTROL EVERYTHING

50 WHAT'S HOLDING YOU BACK?

CONTENTS

52 BEAT THE CURSE OF COMPARISON

55 WHEN GOSSIP IS GOOD

56 WHY DON'T WE PLAY MORE?

60 15 WAYS TO MAKE LIFE MORE FUN

62 THE GREAT ESCAPE

64 THE THRILL OF ANTICIPATION

66 THE WANDERING MIND

70 WHAT IS LOVE?

76 THE GOOD ARGUMENT GUIDE

78 BUILD BETTER RELATIONSHIPS

84 THE POWER OF FRIENDSHIP

90 THE COURAGE TO BE VULNERABLE

96 THE MAGIC OF HUGGING

98 BOOST HAPPINESS WITH DIET AND EXERCISE

102 MEDITATION AND THE BRAIN

108 MODERN MEDITATION

112 LET THE TREES TREAT YOU

114 EMBRACE THE BLUE

118 COULD COLOUR BE THE CURE?

122 WHY DECLUTTERING CAN BOOST YOUR WELLBEING

128 BREAK UP WITH SOCIAL MEDIA

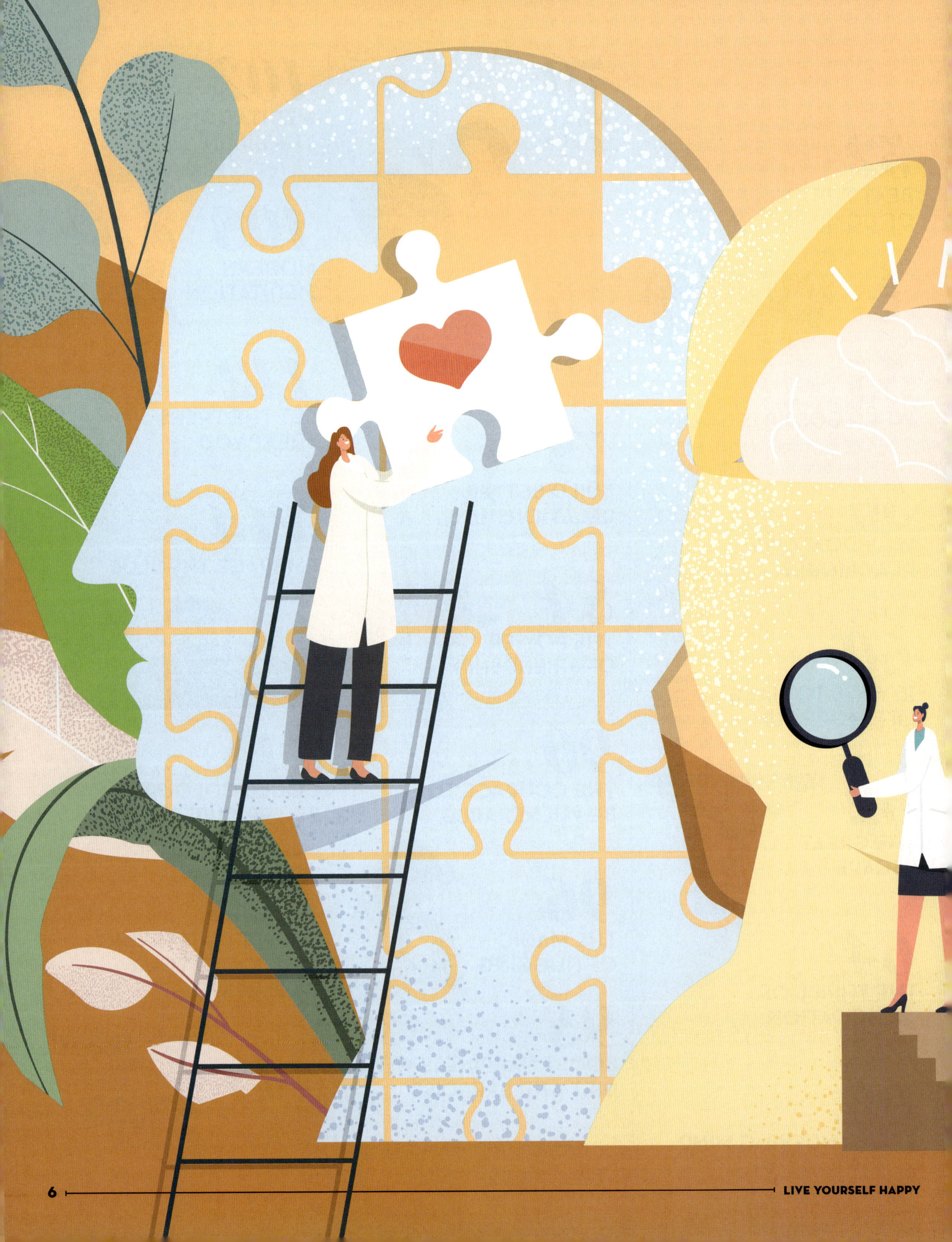

YOUR MENTAL HEALTH MASTERCLASS

YOUR MENTAL HEALTH *Masterclass*

We look after our physical health, but our emotional wellbeing often gets neglected. It's time to make it a priority

WORDS NATALIA LUBOMIRSKI

Despite a staggering one in four people in the UK experiencing a mental health problem each year, the invisible nature of it means there's often a tendency to ignore problems and just get on with it. But, as Stephen Buckley, head of information at mental health charity Mind, says, "Mental health is just like our physical health: everybody has it and we need to take care of it."

He adds, "Thankfully, we've seen the national conversation on mental health move forward, but those with mental health problems still face barriers." The topic remains taboo, especially for older »

> "THE INVISIBLE NATURE OF IT MEANS THERE'S A TENDENCY TO IGNORE PROBLEMS"

LIVE YOURSELF HAPPY

generations – a YouGov survey revealed 25% of over-55s think it's more difficult for them to discuss mental health than younger people. Some 71% felt this was because, in the past, anxiety and depression were seen as weaknesses, rather than health conditions.

ROAD TO RECOVERY

These figures are no surprise, especially after the recent pandemic. But it's how we deal with it that's important. Thankfully, there are things we can do. "Eating healthily, sleeping well, exercising and seeking help are all key," says Stephen. "Different treatments work for different people and the journey to recovery won't always be easy."

Here, Mind shares its advice on three common mental health issues.

DEPRESSION

What is it? In its mildest form, it means being repeatedly in low spirits – at its most severe, it can be life-threatening, making you feel suicidal.
The impact? Symptoms can include "feeling low, numb, worthless or without hope," says Stephen. "You may sleep too much or too little, and withdraw from social contact."
Help yourself List activities, people and places that make you feel good, and try to find ways to bring these things into your daily routine.
Do something new This can boost your mood and break unhelpful patterns of thinking. You could try volunteering – it makes you feel better and less alone.
Try self-help Explore cognitive behavioural therapy.

ANXIETY

What is it? Feeling anxious is a natural response when we feel under threat. But if you regularly experience anxiety, including panic attacks, which are strong, last a long time and are difficult to control, you may need help.
The impact? You avoid situations that may make you feel anxious. You'll find it hard to go about your everyday life or do things you enjoy.
Help yourself focus on breathing, especially during a panic attack. Inhale through your nose and out through your mouth, counting from one to five.
Try complementary and alternative therapies, including meditation, aromatherapy, massage, yoga and reflexology, to aid relaxation.
Not sure if you have a problem? Read on to find out more about the secret signs of anxiety.

OBSESSIVE COMPULSIVE DISORDER (OCD)

What is it? An anxiety disorder with obsessions (unwelcome thoughts, urges and worries that appear in your mind, making you feel anxious) and compulsions (repetitive activities to reduce anxiety, such as checking a door is locked or repeating phrases).
The impact? You might avoid situations that trigger it, including work or seeing friends or family. You may feel ashamed of your thoughts or feel the need to hide your OCD.
Help yourself Talk to someone you trust or write down feelings to discuss together.
Learn to relax Manage stress

> **"IT'S THOUGHT THAT AROUND THREE MILLION PEOPLE IN THE UK HAVE AN ANXIETY DISORDER"**

and try techniques such as deep breathing or mindfulness.
Try peer support This brings together people who have had similar experiences. It helps you feel accepted and confident.

NO MORE FEELING ANXIOUS!

Millions of us are experiencing anxiety, often without even realising it. Most of us probably think we know what anxiety feels like. Your heart races, you're short of breath, and your body is bathed in a sheen of sweat. But there are plenty of hidden signs, too. Follow this advice on how to spot the hidden signs and do something about it.

"Anxiety is what we feel when we are worried, tense or afraid," says Nicky Lidbetter, CEO of Anxiety UK. It can be caused by a number of factors, including feelings of uncertainty, physical health problems, stress, and your childhood experiences. It's thought that around three million people in the UK have an anxiety disorder, and while clammy hands and a pounding heart could signal anxiety, some signs are less obvious. Here are the more subtle symptoms to look out for...

YOU OVER-DRAMATISE SMALL FAILURES

"There's a catastrophising nature to anxiety that makes you perceive things being much worse than they actually are," says Nicky. If you're overdramatic, you may have an over-the-top reaction to a small failing, which could lead to a meltdown or cause you to stay at home for the next few days, unable to face the world.

COULD YOU BE SAD?

Does your mood and energy dip in the winter months? SAD is a mood disorder or depression that comes and goes in a seasonal pattern. Symptoms, including a persistent low mood, anxiety, loss of interest in everyday activities, irritability, feeling lethargic, sleeping for longer, craving carbs and gaining weight, are more apparent during winter. What helps? When it comes to SAD, "the same rules apply as to general depression," says Dr Jeff Foster (drjefffoster.co.uk). He suggests exercise, a healthy diet, reducing alcohol intake, socialising and keeping mentally active as ways to reduce symptoms, as well as getting outside as much as you can during daylight hours.

YOUR MENTAL HEALTH MASTERCLASS

WHAT IS STRESS?

Being under pressure is part of life, and it can help you take action, feel energised and get results. But if you are overwhelmed, these feelings could be a problem. While stress isn't a psychiatric diagnosis, it's closely linked to mental health. Manage external pressures and develop your emotional resilience so you're better at coping, including looking after physical health, giving yourself a break and building support networks.

YOU OVERTHINK
"When you're anxious, you're desperately trying to make sense of a situation. Overthinking and labouring over every eventuality is a way of protecting yourself and gaining control," says Nicky.

YOU'RE AFRAID TO TAKE RISKS
Sticking to your 'comfort zone' means you won't have to face frustration, embarrassment, sadness, anger or disappointment – all extreme feelings for someone with anxiety. "When we're anxious, we want to protect ourselves and can see risks as threats, so we become risk-averse," says Nicky.

YOU TALK TOO MUCH
You may be in a 'high-functioning' state when you're anxious, meaning your mind is going at 100mph. As a result, your actions – such as talking a lot – may follow suit.

YOU'RE CRITICAL OF YOURSELF AND OTHERS
"Being anxious leads to you being hard on yourself. It thrives on the lack of self-esteem you have for yourself and, as a result, you become self-critical and critical of those around you," says Nicky.

YOU CAN'T SLEEP
When we're in an anxious state, it can be hard for our body and mind to relax, and we can have trouble sleeping, which can lead to bouts of insomnia.

YOU'RE DISTRACTED
"We may be preoccupied with our thoughts and easily distracted," says Nicky. Experiencing racing thoughts is common with anxiety, but this attention to the 'inner dialogue' can result in others perceiving us as distant.

> **"BEING ANXIOUS THRIVES ON THE LACK OF SELF-ESTEEM YOU HAVE"**

LIVE YOURSELF HAPPY

YOUR MENTAL HEALTH MASTERCLASS

"TRYING TO HIDE SYMPTOMS FROM OTHERS CAN IMPACT PHYSICAL HEALTH"

YOU'RE UNWILLING TO MAKE FRIENDS
Opening yourself up emotionally can make you feel vulnerable and exposed. You may already be imagining losing that friendship before it's even started. "Anxiety may isolate us by way of protecting ourselves from unknown territory," says Nicky.

YOU FEEL UNWELL
Constant anxiety has a big effect on the immune system, and trying to hide symptoms from others can impact physical health. "Anxiety can make us fatigued and even sick. Plus, adrenaline released can have a negative impact on our stomachs, as well as other parts of the body," explains Nicky.

When it's more serious...
Seek additional help and support if anxiety is disrupting your day-to-day life and stopping you from doing activities you previously enjoyed.

SHORTCUTS TO SERENITY
These quick tips can help, so make sure you practise them daily:

A person who feels they are not worth listening to will speak quickly, because they don't want to keep others waiting on something not worth listening to. A person in authority speaks slowly; even if you don't feel

LIVE YOURSELF HAPPY

YOUR MENTAL HEALTH MASTERCLASS

very confident, try slowing down and see how it feels.

Too much to do? Write down each task you can't do right now on a separate piece of paper. Then, every other day, take a random one and do it. You'll soon get through the list.

Learn to recognise negative self-talk ('I can't run any more, I've got to stop'). Visualise it as an irritating bug, stamp on it, kill it, then replace it with a positive one ('Come on, I can do this! Only half a mile left!').

Laugh often. Watch a funny film or a YouTube video and have a good belly laugh. Science shows it helps to lower the stress hormone cortisol and can shift a low mood.

You are what you do, so if you change what you do, you change what you are. Act in a positive way, take action instead of telling yourself you can't. Talk to people in a positive way. You'll soon start to notice a difference.

If you choose to say 'no' to something, mentally rehearse the conversation beforehand, saying it simply and directly, giving no more than one key reason. Do not get into explaining or arguing: just repeat 'No, because…' quietly and firmly.

Before always saying 'yes' to demands, take a deep breath, so you can touch base with yourself to discover what you would truly, honestly prefer to do.

Have a list of useful apps that benefit your mental health. Try Headspace, Stress & Anxiety Companion, and Catch It.

Don't aim too high. Set a goal you know you can achieve, then achieve it. You'll feel good. Now set another and achieve that. Soon you'll be setting bigger goals and achieving those, too.

Visualise yourself at your most confident, then link this feeling to a physical action, such as pinching your thumb and forefinger together. Next time you need to feel confident in a situation, pinch your thumb and finger together to get back to that positive mental state.

Keep talking. Having a chat with a loved one, sending a text to a friend, or asking your colleague to go for a walk is the best tonic for a low mood.

Standing tall and straight makes you feel better about yourself. Imagine a piece of string is pulling the top of your head towards the sky, and the rest of your body straightens accordingly.

Immerse yourself in nature. So-called 'green therapy', being outdoors is a powerful mood-lifter. A Stanford University study showed that a 90-minute walk in nature reduced ruminations, which is a risk factor for mental illness.

HOW TO BE CALM

"If you're feeling anxious, there are ways you can step back and take control before the symptoms build up and take over," says Nicky.

DO A BREATHING EXERCISE
Breathe in through the nose for three seconds, hold for four seconds, breathe out through the mouth slowly for five seconds.

USE A DISTRACTION TECHNIQUE
Try the 5, 4, 3, 2, 1 technique – acknowledge five things you can see, four things you can hear, three things you can touch, two things you can smell, and finally one deep breath in and out.

TRY POSITIVE AFFIRMATIONS
Tell yourself, 'I am safe, I am in control, this feeling is anxiety', and repeat until you feel more in control of your feelings.

MAKE DIETARY CHANGES
Small changes to your diet can make a difference to anxiety symptoms. Try eating less processed food, drinking less alcohol, and cutting back or stopping caffeine. Don't forget that caffeine can be present in chocolate and soft drinks, too.

GET ENOUGH SLEEP
Maintain a regular sleeping pattern by going to bed at the same time each night, switching off screens at least one hour before bedtime, and ensuring your bedroom is dark and the right temperature.

LIVE YOURSELF HAPPY

WHICH *therapy* IS FOR ME?

There's a multitude of problems therapy can help with and just as many approaches to take. How do you know which is right for you?

WHICH THERAPY IS FOR ME?

WORDS SARA NIVEN

PSYCHODYNAMIC PSYCHOTHERAPY

Stemming from Sigmund Freud's psychoanalysis, Freud believed that psychological problems are rooted in the unconscious mind, and experiences from a person's past can influence their thoughts and behaviour in later life. Positive change is seen as happening as a result of uncovering repressed events and linking them to present difficulties. You might spend significant time discussing your childhood or recalling dreams, with your therapist suggesting connections. This approach also emphasises the idea and exploration of transference, where feelings you experienced in previous relationships may be projected onto your therapist – for example, you view them as a critical teacher or favourite uncle.
Suitable for A wide range of issues, including depression and anxiety.
Considerations Some people might prefer to focus on the present than revisit their childhood. Therapy may take place over a longer time frame than some other approaches.

PERSON-CENTRED THERAPY

This form of therapy falls into a category called 'humanistic', where the client is seen as able to solve difficulties themselves, given the right conditions. Developed by psychologist Carl Rogers in the 1940s, there is an emphasis on the counsellor showing unconditional positive regard (UPR), which refers to non-judgemental warmth and acceptance. The therapist aims to ensure a client feels heard and understood, and enables them to lead the session and set the pace. Compared to a psychodynamic counsellor, a person-centred one is more likely to occasionally reveal their own experiences (self-disclosure) if they see it as helpful for emphasising understanding.
Suitable for All ages and a wide range of issues, including grief, depression, anxiety and stress.
Considerations The outcome of person-centred therapy depends on what a client chooses to talk about in sessions. Some people might want more directive help than this form of counselling typically provides.

GESTALT THERAPY

Gestalt therapy is another form of humanistic therapy based on the belief in a client's natural ability to achieve healthy balance and growth. Developed by psychotherapists Fritz and Laura Perls, it places a strong focus on immediacy in addition to the client/counsellor relationship.
Although any skilled therapist will pay attention to your body language, a Gestalt therapist is more likely to comment on this. They might tell you they notice you tapping your feet when discussing a particular topic, for instance, and encourage you to »

> "SOME PREFER TO FOCUS ON THE PRESENT THAN REVISIT CHILDHOOD"

LIVE YOURSELF HAPPY

> **"A CBT THERAPIST WILL BE MORE DIRECTIVE AND ENCOURAGE YOU TO CHALLENGE NEGATIVE BELIEFS"**

consider what that means. There might also be aspects of role playing and creativity, using pebbles or other objects. The 'empty chair' is a well-known Gestalt technique where a client is encouraged to address a chair as though someone they have an unresolved issue with is sitting there.
Suitable for Issues including anxiety, depression, low self-esteem and relationship problems.
Considerations Some people enjoy the more creative techniques used in Gestalt therapy, while others might feel uncomfortable. As with any form of counselling, feeling safe and having a good level of trust with your therapist is key.

COGNITIVE BEHAVIOURAL THERAPY (CBT)

CBT falls under the category of behavioural therapy and is goal orientated. A CBT therapist will be more directive and encourage you to challenge and change negative or outdated beliefs that are causing difficulties. They might also set 'homework' to do between sessions.

This could be a good approach for conquering a specific fear, such as starting to drive again after a road accident. While a person-centred counsellor would focus on empathy and understanding, a CBT therapist would be aiming to uncover the beliefs and fears you have about this, challenge these and take steps towards overcoming them.
Suitable for In addition to depression and anxiety, CBT can be used to treat obsessive compulsive disorder (OCD), phobias and substance abuse issues.

Considerations Therapy tends to be focused on specific goals and outcomes and is often relatively short term. Exposure therapy (where you confront situations you generally avoid) can be challenging.

DIALECTICAL BEHAVIOURAL THERAPY (DBT)

An adaptation of CBT, which uses some of the same skills, DBT was developed in the 1970s and is aimed at people who struggle with very intense emotions. For this reason, it is the therapy of choice for treating people diagnosed with borderline personality disorder (BPD). Like CBT, it focuses on change but there is more of an emphasis on mindfulness and learning how to regulate emotions and tolerate distress without turning to harmful coping mechanisms.
Suitable for Mental health conditions, including BPD, self-harm, eating issues, addiction and PTSD.
Considerations People undergoing DBT might be asked to commit to more than just one-to-one sessions – group skills training, phone coaching and homework could also be involved.

TRANSACTIONAL ANALYSIS (TA)

Transactional analysis focuses on the way you relate to others, be that your partner, your boss or a family member. Developed by psychiatrist Eric Berne in the late 1950s, it divides the human personality into three basic ego states: parent (with nurturing and critical sides), adult and child. This aims to increase our understanding of interacting with others and the responses we get, such as regularly being in critical parent mode when speaking to your partner, which then results in conflict.

TA therapists also look at our beliefs in terms of 'scripts' and help a client re-evaluate any unhelpful ones formed while growing up, which are impacting negatively on them, for example, 'I must never make a mistake'.
Suitable for A range of issues, including relationship difficulties, low self-esteem and workplace challenges. TA is often applied outside of the therapy room, for example in coaching or educational situations.
Considerations Supporters of TA cite the simple models and language, which are much easier than some other theories for clients to understand and apply to everyday situations.

EYE MOVEMENT DESENSITISATION REPROCESSING THERAPY (EMDR)

Developed by a psychologist called Francine Shapiro in the late 1980s, EMDR aims to help the brain to reprocess traumatic memories. Clients won't lose the memory but ideally it should not continue to trigger such strong emotions.

EMDR has a specific structure, with eight stages that a therapist works through with you. After the initial stages, therapy involves activating a disturbing memory while introducing what is called bilateral stimulation (BLS) involving eye movements, physical tapping or other stimuli to activate both sides of the brain.
Suitable for EMDR is recognised by the World Health Organization (WHO) as a treatment for post-traumatic stress disorder (PTSD). It can also be used for a range of other issues, such as unresolved grief and mental illnesses, including personality disorders.
Considerations Talking about difficult memories in detail isn't seen as a significant part of the process, which could be helpful for people keen to avoid that, although they will be asked to recall experiences. This therapy isn't considered suitable for clients with substance abuse issues.

ART THERAPY

As the name suggests, this form of psychotherapy uses art as a form of communication and way of addressing difficult emotions. Complex emotions can be put onto paper or canvas, and creating and discussing the resulting art with a therapist can help give clients clarity over intense but confused feelings and connect with their unconscious mind.
Suitable for Art therapy can be used by people in a wide range of situations, including physical illnesses, such as cancer, learning disabilities, eating disorders and dementia. It can also be used with children.
Considerations You don't need to be a budding Michelangelo or Monet to have art therapy – no artistic skills are necessary; however, some people may feel less comfortable than others expressing themselves in this way. A skilled therapist should provide plenty of opportunity to work through the emotions the art session brings up.

INTEGRATIVE THERAPY

Rather than specialising in one, many therapists now train in a range of different therapeutic approaches and use these like tools in a toolbox, to be taken out according to what seems most useful at the time. One week they might work in an entirely person-centred way, allowing the client to lead the session. Another time, they might outline the ego states that are part of TA theory to help the client gain insight into a relationship difficulty, or draw on Gestalt training to suggest the 'empty chair' exercise.

Suitable for Integrative therapy is increasingly common and seen as suitable for many issues including bereavement, relationship difficulties and eating disorders.

Considerations This is a more 'bespoke,' form of therapy with less structure than some others, but shouldn't be experienced as confusing or completely random. Integrative therapists work to tailor their approach to a client's needs, not use different ones just for the sake of variety.

HYPNOTHERAPY

Hypnotherapy isn't a theoretical approach or considered a traditional talking therapy that falls under the remit of the British Association of Counselling and Psychotherapy or the American Counseling Association.

However, there is evidence that it can be an effective form of treatment for anxiety and anxiety-related disorders, such as headaches and irritable bowel syndrome, while others report finding it helpful in addressing a range of other difficulties.

During sessions, hypnosis combined with talking therapy aims to work on both a conscious and subconscious level, to bring about positive change while adjustments can be made to limiting beliefs that have influenced or directed the client's life.

Suitable for Anxiety, phobias, addictions, low self-esteem, insomnia and stress-related conditions.

Considerations Hypnotherapy isn't advised if you have psychosis or a personality disorder. As with any form of therapy, it is important to ensure a hypnotherapist is suitably trained and check them out with the relevant regulatory body.

Whatever therapy you opt for, it is essential your therapist is properly qualified and works to professional standards. In the UK, the best way to establish this is via the **British Association for Counselling and Psychotherapy (BACP)** (www.bacp.co.uk/about-therapy/how-to-find-a-therapist), and in the US, the **American Counseling Association (ACA)**. (www.counseling.org/aca-community/learn-about-counseling/what-is-counseling/find-a-counselor)

HOW TO STRESS *Better*

You can't escape it entirely, but stress isn't all bad, and there are ways to harness it to your advantage

HOW TO STRESS BETTER

WORDS JENNY ROWE

As the cost of living crisis spirals, our stress levels are following suit. One in five people in the UK say they feel stressed more than they don't, and money worries are one of the primary causes*. But we shouldn't be scared of stress. "It's normal," says psychotherapist Caron Barruw, co-founder of The Niche Group. "It's how we manage it that makes the difference."

We can learn to turn stress into something more useful – helpful even, adds neuroscientist and author of *Psycho-Logical*, Dr Dean Burnett. Sound good? Here's how to harness and not hate all stress.

A helping hand
"Stress is the brain's threat detection system preparing us to deal with danger," says Dr Burnett. It mostly feels unpleasant, but on a fundamental level it keeps us safe. "While it is usually the consequence of a negative situation, there may be positive outcomes," says Caron. This is more likely if we are working towards a goal that we believe is positive too, such as interviewing for a new job, getting married or running a race.

Ultimately, an optimal dose of stress can help us perform better. "The stress response increases muscle tension and raises heart and breathing rate, which makes you more focused, less distractible and more motivated," says Dr Burnett. Whatever you're feeling stressed about, this physiological reaction means you are more likely to complete the task to the best of your ability. This is stress in its positive form, which is known as eustress.

Striking a balance
"Countless studies have shown that, up to a point, a person's performance increases directly in proportion to how much stress they're experiencing," says Dr Burnett. However, if stress levels continue past this point, we start to struggle. "This increases our stress levels again and we can get stuck in a stress cycle," says Caron.

The main issue with stress is when you have too much of it for too long – this is when acute stress morphs into chronic, more harmful stress. "When stress is constant, it's like keeping your foot on the accelerator," says Caron. "It leads to burnout."

Breaking point
Stress is sneaky. It can be easy to keep cruising through life, not realising you're approaching burnout – until you're there. "Our brains aren't particularly good at noticing changes that happen over long periods," says Dr Burnett. "But it can be done, particularly if the changes caused by stress are marked."

You may be struggling to sleep, have low or high appetite, headaches, low sexual desire or high blood pressure. If you are unable to finish tasks, feel tearful, worry all the time or snap at people when you normally wouldn't, then stress may be affecting your wellbeing and it's time to get help.

It's important to recognise that there is a difference between coping with stress and dealing with it. "Dealing with stress involves processing stressful emotions and actively bringing about changes that address the cause of stress," says Dr Burnett. "Coping is just putting up with the stressful situation and carrying on, which is not a great long-term strategy, as our capacity for tolerating stress will max out eventually."

How to stress better
So can we become better at dealing with stress and stop it tipping us over the edge? In short, yes. Like musicians, dancers and actors who are taught to reinterpret their nerves as excitement, it's possible to change our emotional reactions to stressful experiences into something more positive – though obviously this depends on the situation, and mainly applies to small-scale day-to-day dramas.

Optimists who choose to see potential daily stressors (such as traffic jams and chores) as challenges rather than threats before emotions flare up, reduce the negative impact of stress, as shown in a recent two-decade-long study**.

You can also try to increase your threshold for stress. "By taking on new challenges and pushing yourself beyond your comfort zone – but in ways that you feel OK with – you could gradually increase the amount of stress you're capable of dealing with," says Dr Burnett.

KNOW YOUR STRESSORS

To stress better (and less), we need to know our triggers. Stress trackers monitor things like heart rate variability (the variation in time between each heart beat) to measure stress levels and help us identify our personal triggers – so we can come up with solutions. The key to successful stress tracking is to ensure you're asking, 'Why am I stressed?', not the less useful question, 'How stressed am I?', says Dr Burnett.
TRY IT Most fitness wearables now have stress tracking capabilities, or you can try the StressScan app for free (Apple, Google Play). At its simplest, stress tracking could just mean keeping a stress diary. "Rate the stress from 1-10 as it happens," says Caron. "This will help you feel in control of the stress rather than the stress controlling you."

> **"WE CAN LEARN TO TURN STRESS INTO SOMETHING MORE USEFUL"**

*Ciphr. **The Journals of Gerontology

PANICKED? PRESS PAUSE

PANICKED? PRESS PAUSE

PANICKED?
Press Pause

It's easier than you think to take back control when you're having a panic attack

WORDS ROSE GOODMAN

A pounding heart, crushing chest pain and debilitating terror may sound like the signs of a heart attack, but for those who suffer from panic attacks, these scary symptoms are all too common. Sound familiar? You're not alone – up to a third of people will experience at least one panic attack in their lifetime*, while others will have regular attacks or several in a short space of time.

Whatever your experience, there are ways to bring a panic attack under control. Here, our experts explain what could help...

What happens?
"A panic attack is an intense emotional and physical response to a sense of dread or fear," says psychologist Dr Alison McClymont. "It may have an obvious trigger (such as being under stress), but it may also come on seemingly unprovoked and can make you feel as if your health – or, in extreme situations, your life – is under threat."

Spot the signs
The overwhelming symptom of a panic attack is a sense of impending doom or anxiety. "This may be accompanied by difficulty breathing (hyperventilating), sweaty palms, a racing heart or muscle pain," explains Dr McClymont. Trembling, dizziness and feeling detached from reality are also common symptoms.

The physical symptoms can be so extreme that some sufferers may go to A&E, believing they are having a heart »

SUPPORTING A LOVED ONE

If you're with someone who is experiencing a panic attack, it can be difficult to know how to help. But there are some simple ways you can help make them feel safe and at ease. "Don't touch them. Speak calmly and slowly, remind them where they are, that they are safe, and that you are there," says Dr McClymont. "Try modelling slow, calm breathing (in for four and out for eight), get them some water and keep reminding them that this will pass, and that breathing is the key."

LIVE YOURSELF HAPPY

PANICKED? PRESS PAUSE

5 WAYS TO PREVENT AN ATTACK

These daily habits can help to reduce future panic attacks, says the Mental Health Foundation:

• Practise better breathing (do the 4-7-8 breathing technique daily).

• *Take regular exercise, such as walking or yoga. This will help to reduce stress and improve your mood.*

• Eat frequent meals to stabilise blood-sugar levels.

• *Avoid caffeine, alcohol and smoking.*

• Try mindfulness to bring you back to the present moment. Download the Calm app (*£7.99/$14.99 per month, iOS and Android*).

---

attack. However, while panic attacks are frightening, they're not dangerous and won't cause you physical harm.

Stay calm
If you feel a panic attack developing, try to think of it like a big wave. You cannot stop it, but you can ride it. "Distract yourself from catastrophic thoughts and don't buy into them," says Dr Paul McLaren, consultant psychiatrist for the Priory Group. There are also things you can do to take back a feeling of control.

JUST BREATHE
"Try to slow your breathing, even though you will feel that you need to breathe harder," says Dr McLaren. This 4-7-8 breathing exercise will help activate your parasympathetic nervous system, which is responsible for relaxation.

1. Close your mouth and inhale through your nose for a count of four.

2. Now hold your breath for a count of seven.

3. Exhale completely out of your mouth, making a 'whoosh' sound, for a count of eight.

4. Inhale again and repeat the cycle three more times, or more if needed.

GROUND YOURSELF
Try the 5,4,3,2,1 grounding technique, which will bring you back to the present moment. This exercise requires you to engage all of your senses by naming:

Five things you can see.

Four things you feel, such as the texture of a chair or the temperature of the room you're in.

Three things you can hear.

Two things you can smell.

One thing you can taste. If you can't taste anything, name a taste you like.

NOTICE YOUR BODY
A body-scan exercise can release tension you're not even aware you're holding. Practising this technique regularly can help reduce anxiety, depression and fatigue. During a panic attack, doing this exercise can help to bring you back to your body and feel safe within it. Give it a go:

Sit or lie down in a comfortable spot and position.

Start with the breathing strategy described in the previous column and then focus on your toes.

Check in with what you can feel and how they feel. Give them a little wiggle.

Move on to the soles of your feet. Keep breathing slowly and gradually move up through your body, checking in, moving and relaxing each part as you go.

When you've completed this, gradually go back down your body in the same order whilst continuing your slow and steady breath style. This can be a really useful activity to help you de-stress and be more mindful and body aware.

IMAGINE A SAFE SPACE
Also known as visualisation, this technique requires you to imagine that you're in a calm, safe and soothing place. "Think about what you can see, hear, taste, smell and feel," says clinical psychologist Dr Marianne Trent, creator of The Feel Better Academy. "Know that you can revisit this place in your mind whenever you choose." Your safe space could be anywhere – from a tropical beach or your garden in the summer, to a relaxing bubble bath.

BE AWARE
Feeling stressed out? Integrative counsellor Katharina Wolf suggests using a technique called AWARE, which works to move your brain from a state of high anxiety to a place of calm, and helps to avoid creating further triggers.

Accept the anxiety/panic. Fighting it will only heighten it.

Watch and scale your panic/anxiety from one to ten (with ten being maximum panic/anxiety).

Act normally, while imagining yourself calm.

Repeat the above three steps.

Expect the best. Use positive statements such as, 'This can't harm me'; 'I can master this'; 'This will go away soon'.

Rest and recover
It's common to feel exhausted and emotional after suffering a panic attack. "Go to a calm and quiet place. Play some music and take time to comfort yourself and re-engage with your surroundings," advises Dr McClymont. "Drink water and, if you feel dizzy, try eating a small amount of sugar. The most important thing is to be still, breathe, and show yourself

compassion for the intense and frightening experience you have just endured"

Panic attack or anxiety attack?
While these terms are often used interchangeably, the symptoms of a panic attack and an anxiety attack do differ slightly. "An anxiety attack is usually not accompanied by such a sense of impending doom or death," says Dr McClymont. "The physical symptoms are similar, but in a panic attack the threat response is more highly elevated and things such as hyperventilating or chest pain are more likely to occur."

Stop the cycle
Talking therapies such as cognitive behavioural therapy (CBT) are often used to treat panic attacks. "It is likely that panic developed for an important reason to protect you from something painful or difficult, says Dr Trent. "Working through these reasons and learning more about why you respond in the way you do can be incredibly useful, and enable you to enjoy your life more fully."

> **IT'S COMMON TO FEEL EXHAUSTED AND EMOTIONAL AFTER SUFFERING A PANIC ATTACK**

Is it panic disorder?
If you experience panic attacks, it doesn't necessarily mean that you have panic disorder. As Dr McClymont explains, panic disorder is classified as having at least one panic attack and subsequent fear or intrusive thoughts about having another, across one month.

If you're resorting to unhealthy coping mechanisms or ways of preventing an attack – for example, avoiding certain situations that have caused you anxiety in the past – you may be diagnosed with panic disorder. However, this can only be diagnosed by a professional and may require both medication and therapy to treat it, so visit your doctor if you are concerned.

'I BEAT THE FEAR'

Dr Sophie Mort, clinical psychologist and the author of *A Manual For Being Human*** (£14.99/$18.50, Simon & Schuster), shares her experience of overcoming panic attacks…
"I had my first panic attack aged 18, when I was on holiday. I kept telling myself I had sunstroke, which was why I overheated and my heart was racing. Then the next day it came back, over and over. I knew then that it wasn't the sun.
My panic attacks then escalated to the point where I didn't leave the house for nearly three months, as everything I did set them off. I quit university and didn't see friends.
I finally saw a therapist and she taught me techniques to manage the panic. After a month, I noticed that the attacks had lessened enough for me to leave the house. I haven't had a panic attack in years, and I manage my anxiety with yoga, mindfulness and breathing exercises.
My favourite technique is saying 'bring it on' whenever I feel the physical sensations of anxiety or panic building. That's been the most important part of my journey, because when I say it and really mean it, it removes the fear cycle that kept the panic alive."

*Bupa UK. **Follow Dr Soph on Instagram @_drsopH

MAKE ME-TIME A MUST-DO

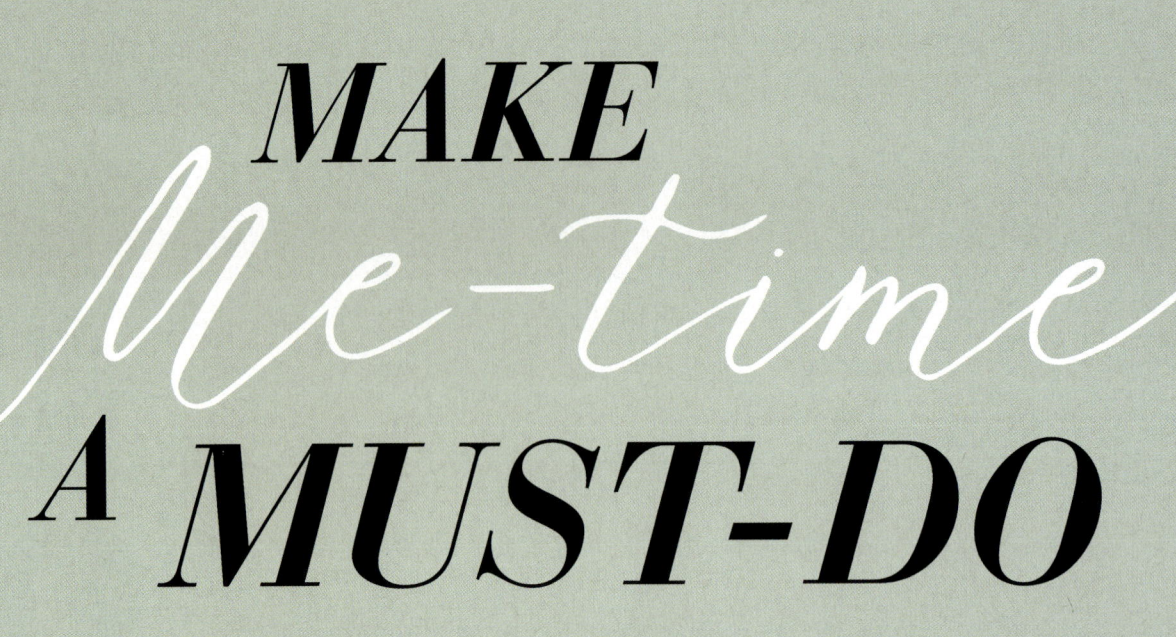

MAKE
Me-time
A MUST-DO

Feeling frazzled? By making a small amount of time for yourself, you'll be instantly refreshed – and happier

WORDS SHARON WALKER

When did you last have time to yourself? When 'mum's taxi' went on strike? The laundrette was off duty? The café you run alongside your *actual* job shut up shop? If that's the sound of your frazzled laugh, we're not surprised. But this is no laughing matter. Time to unwind is "like fuel in the tank," says

> ❝ WE'RE NOT MEANT TO BE DOING AND THINKING ALL OF THE TIME; WE'RE NOT MACHINES ❞

psychologist Dr Jessamy Hibberd. "You need 'self-care' to function at your best," she adds. "We're not meant to be doing and thinking all of the time; we're not machines."

Me-time isn't sitting in a bath surrounded by candles (although it can be). Self-care means going for a walk, meeting a friend or staying in bed; whatever you need to reboot. "Tune in to how you feel and go with it," suggests life coach Jayne Morris. The key is little and often.

Research shows that the resting brain is anything but idle. Downtime gives us time to process unresolved tensions and to gain perspective. Most of us can't simply down

LIVE YOURSELF HAPPY

MAKE ME-TIME A MUST-DO

DR JESSAMY HIBBERD
Dr Hibberd is a psychologist and co-author of the *This Book Will...* series.

JAYNE MORRISR
Jayne is a life coach and author of *Burnout to Brilliance*.

SUZY READING
Suzy is a psychologist and author of *The Self-Care Revolution*.

tools and nip off to a spa. But it *is* possible to carve out time for yourself. Here's how.

How to build your 'me-time muscle' in one minute

If you have one minute to spare at the bus stop or between work calls, put your phone on airplane mode and recharge with a hand massage. Stash a tube of your favourite lotion in your handbag and grab a moment whenever you can. First, rub a few drops into your hand to soften the skin. Use your thumb to work into the fleshy heel of your hand, palm side up, then flip your hand over and work into the web of tendons between your thumb and fingers, moving gently up and down to release tension. Next, move on to the joint at the base of each finger, massaging all the way to the tip. A hand massage is a really good stress-buster for anyone who taps away on a keyboard all day, but it's also the perfect me-time hack if you're standing in a queue or on public transport. "Smell is a powerful mood alchemist," says psychologist Suzy Reading.

TIP
Follow your hand massage with a simple breathing exercise, recommends Dr Hibberd. Breathe in for the count of four, hold for five, and out for six... and repeat.

10 minutes

Carve out 10 minutes for yourself by turning any daily activity into a meditation, whether that's taking a shower or getting ready for work. A simple shower can feel like a full spa treatment if you immerse yourself in the experience rather than worrying about to-do lists. Concentrate on the drops of water hitting your skin and use a deliciously uplifting body scrub to add extra zing. Reading suggests you can turn getting dressed into an act of self-care too. Forget grabbing a bunch of scrunched-up clothes from the back of your wardrobe – instead, take ten minutes to lay out your outfit carefully, picking out colours that lift your spirits.

TIP
For a relaxing break, eat a square of dark chocolate with a cup of hot tea – and don't do anything else. Focus on the taste, texture and smell, relishing the experience – and no multi-tasking! If you really must do something, write a list of the experiences, relationships and emotions you are grateful for.

20 minutes

Perhaps you're sitting on the train or waiting for an appointment – now's your chance to master the art of savouring. This is a lovely mind-wandering trick that Suzy Reading recommends, where you simply start to anticipate everything you're looking forward to, whether that's a coffee with a friend, a party or a holiday. You might also want to dip in to your mental archives to unleash some sunny memories. Researchers at Southampton University found that the odd detour down memory lane can significantly lift your spirits, and those who wrote about »

> ## "IT'S THE PERFECT ME-TIME HACK IF YOU'RE STANDING IN A QUEUE OR ON PUBLIC TRANSPORT"

LIVE YOURSELF HAPPY

MAKE ME-TIME A MUST-DO

> " PICK SOMETHING THAT'S SPECIAL TO YOU AND WILL TAKE YOUR MIND OFF YOUR WORRIES "

happy memories were happier after the exercise than those who didn't. But you don't need a notebook to do this, as the biggest mood spikes come by replaying happy memories in your head. "This kind of nourishment is accessible anywhere, at any time," says Reading. Focus on how positive you felt at the time of the experience, rather than how it's over now to stop the memories from feeling too poignant.

TIP
Make a 'happy times' photo album. Try to think about what happened outside the frame, before and after the photograph was taken – research shows that this gives the most uplifting effect. And share the album with the family and friends you were with. This will spark an opportunity to reminisce and boost the bond that already exists between you.

One hour
If you're at home, or work for a forward-thinking company, take a nap. That extra 40 winks will reduce anxiety, boost concentration and increase your energy. You'll also make wiser food choices, improve your memory and think more clearly. Jayne Morris recommends keeping a small pillow in your desk drawer (she used to bed down in empty meeting rooms when she worked for the BBC), and setting an alarm so you don't 'oversleep'. 15 minutes is best, according to sleep researcher Professor Jim Horne; any longer and you could descend into deep sleep and wake up groggy. If you can't make this happen, move your body instead. Go for a walk or try a yoga class in your lunch hour. You can always take a nap in the back row of the class if you're really shattered (another of Morris's 40-winks tricks). "Just warn the teacher you're taking a rest, so they don't worry there's something wrong," she says. If you work near a swimming pool, Morris recommends a dip as the most nurturing exercise. "There's an association with the womb, when all our needs were catered for, so it feels very soothing."

TIP
Block out an hour before bed to create a wind-down routine. Log out from social media, have a bath, listen to music or read. "I write a list of the good things that have happened," says Dr Hibberd. "It reminds you of what you have and helps you appreciate your life instead of worrying about what you don't have or haven't achieved."

An afternoon
If you're thinking you'll use your free afternoon to clear that email backlog – stop! See a friend instead; it will be better for your health and happiness. "Making time for friends and family is an important part of self-care," says Dr Hibberd. We're social creatures and need relationships like we need air and water. Don't want company? Go somewhere green – and take your shoes off. Yes, really. There's nothing like walking barefoot on the grass to put a spring in your step, believes Morris. "The moment we put our feet on the earth we become more aware of our breath. The deeper we breathe, the clearer we can think." And there's science to back this up. According to research at Harvard Medical School, breathing deeply helps re-oxygenate our cells, which in turn regulates our hormones.

TIP
Too many worries running around in your head? "Go to the cinema," says Dr Hibberd. "It's virtually impossible to do anything else at the same time; you can properly switch off and become absorbed in the film."

A day
Take a quiet moment, close your eyes and focus inwards. Now ask yourself what would be the most beneficial way for you to spend your day. "Just see what comes," says Morris. You might want to connect with a friend, or if you're always with people – as working parents often are – solitude might be what you need. Dr Hibberd suggests planning a fun adventure, perhaps a day out to see a new art exhibition or a trip to the seaside. Pick something that's special to you and will take your mind off your worries. You might want to use the time to reset your priorities. Morris recommends taking five Post-its and writing down the five things most important to you, whether that's work, friends, family or hobbies. Put them in order of importance, then reorder according to the time you spend on each. "People often find work is number one in terms of time, but that might be the least important of their priorities," says Morris. "This shows where things are out of whack and you can spend some time thinking about how you can change your situation."

TIP
Block this time out in your diary and tell work and family that you'll be out of reach except for emergencies. That way – hopefully – they'll think twice before disturbing you.

FIND YOUR *Mantra*

Focus your mind and learn how to reverse negative thought patterns by repeating powerful phrases

WORDS ALI HORSFALL

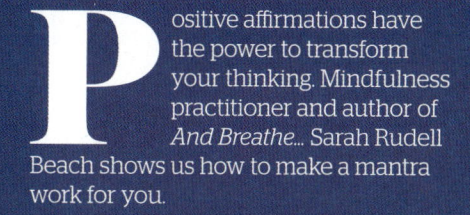

Positive affirmations have the power to transform your thinking. Mindfulness practitioner and author of *And Breathe...* Sarah Rudell Beach shows us how to make a mantra work for you.

Words of wisdom
Mantras are words and phrases that can focus your mind and reverse negative thought patterns. "You can silently repeat them in your head whenever you need them throughout the day, or say them out loud if you find it helpful," says Sarah. "Once you discover the mantras that most resonate with you, write them down on a Post-it, or on your favourite stationery, and put them where you'll see them regularly such as on a mirror or your fridge."

Say it with ease
When choosing an affirmation it should feel comfortable and appropriate for the internal thoughts that you want to quieten. 'I don't need to be perfect', 'I will look for the good', or 'I will focus on what I can control', are good examples. "If a mantra doesn't feel right to you," says Sarah, "modify it."

> ❝ DISCOVER THE MANTRAS THAT RESONATE WITH YOU ❞

TRY THESE POWER PHRASES DURING YOUR DAY

MORNING AFFIRMATION
'I'll handle what today brings'
"When we get upset because things don't go to plan, it's often because we weren't aware of our plan in the first place," says Sarah. Think about what you're expecting today, so you can skilfully meet the moments that don't deliver.

MIDDAY REMINDER
'I can do this'
When things get tough during your day, repeat this mantra. "You've done hard things before. Know that whatever it is you're facing, you already have everything you need to handle it," Sarah explains. "You have your presence, your attention, and your breath. You've got this."

EVENING MANTRA
'I did my best today'
Use this mantra before bed. "Reflect on what was good," says Sarah, "what was hard, and who you helped or who helped you."

WHY WE SHOULD ALL BE MORE *Selfish*

Putting yourself first has more benefits to you and even the people around you than you might realise

WORDS SARAH BANKES

From a very young age, we're told to be kind, to share, to see things from other people's viewpoints, to put others first and to be polite, amongst many other life lessons. And while these are important skills to learn – equipping us with qualities that turn us into decent human beings – taking these instructions to the extreme can actually be detrimental to our own mental health and wellbeing.

As children, we probably remember our parents coming out with the following sorts of phrases (and as parents we're probably guilty of repeating these to our own children):

"Give Grandpa a kiss goodbye, go on, don't be rude…"

> **PRIORITISING YOUR NEEDS CAN BENEFIT EVERYONE INVOLVED**

"I know you don't like mushrooms, but we're guests, so eat up…"

Telling kids to do things they really don't want to do doesn't make us bad parents – nor does it make our parents wicked for doing the same – but it does send out a message that other people's feelings are more important than our own. Coupled with the idea that to be selfish is a negative trait, we're brought up to believe that to be a good person, we must at all times be selfless, altruistic and self-sacrificing, and these beliefs lead to a whole host of problems.

We can't blame our parents for everything, though. A study carried out in 2016/17 by a team from University of California, Los Angeles suggests that altruistic behaviour might actually be the default option in our brains. According to their research, an area of the prefrontal cortex can be specifically affected to make people less giving.

What's wrong with being selfless?
Excessive selflessness leads to an inability to say no. We live

WHY WE SHOULD ALL BE MORE SELFISH

in fear of appearing rude and upsetting or offending people. As we go about our lives pleasing everybody else, if we don't burn out first, we run the risk of ultimately becoming bitter, resentful and pretty unhappy, as prioritising everybody else leaves little time to do the things we want to do.

Perhaps a distinction needs to be made between good and bad versions of selfishness. A total disregard for other people's feelings isn't always necessary when it comes to putting yourself first. However, being aware of your needs and being assertive enough to prioritise them can benefit everyone involved.

For example, a friend asks you to go shopping and, even though you already have a busy schedule and want to say no, you say yes because you don't want to let her down. What happens? You end up being late because you're squeezing it in around other things. Consequently you're stressed before you've even stepped foot inside a shop; you spend the entire trip annoyed with your friend for 'dragging you along', when actually you could have said no; and you're anxious about the next commitment in your jam-packed diary! What would the outcome have been if you'd said no? You'd feel less stressed, for sure, you'd have more time to focus on the other things you're doing that day, and you wouldn't resent your friend. And the friend? She might initially feel somewhat put out, but she wouldn't have to put up with a late, grumpy, stressed-out shopping companion! Being supposedly 'selfless' isn't always beneficial to the people you think you're helping out.

More often than not, the issue goes far deeper than wanting to please other people for *their* sake. If you'd considered the shopping situation rationally and truthfully, the friend could probably have found someone else to go with, so the real issue was perhaps not so much not wanting to let her down, but more about not wanting her to be disappointed in you. Being a people-pleaser is usually a result of seeking approval or wanting to be liked, which is often a consequence of previous life events.

Stress and anxiety are just two of the consequences of being excessively selfless. If you don't start prioritising your needs, you become ineffective at what you're trying to be, whether that's a good friend, a reliable employee or a good parent. This can then lead to low self-esteem, depression and burnout. Taking time out from the kids might feel like an indulgence but if a one-hour bubble bath is what you need to unwind and destress, your kids are going to be much happier with a relaxed parent than one who is trying to do everything for everyone, and not giving themselves a well-earned break.

Over the coming days and weeks, try to focus on prioritising your needs and setting boundaries.

THE GIFT OF COMPASSION

THE GIFT OF
Compassion

Many of us find it hard to treat ourselves with the kindness and compassion we willingly give to others, but it's essential we do it

WORDS CLAIRE CANTOR

Compassion is the willingness to help others, show kindness and caring when they are suffering, and try to help relieve their pain. 'Self'-compassion is offering that kindness to yourself.

We are our own worst enemy. Blaming and criticising ourselves, telling ourselves we should be better/do more/achieve more. If we don't match up to our standards and rules of living, the self-bullying only gets worse.

We understand that beating ourselves up is counterproductive. Yet we reserve our understanding for others. We consider self-nurturing as indulgent, and worry we may take our foot off the pedal and let ourselves go. No one can convince us that we *too* are worthy of love. No new job, another person, or attaining our 'ideal' weight is going to change how we feel about ourselves. Offering ourselves self-compassion can help to relieve us from the self-defeating messages. Follow these steps to get started.

NOTICE AND ACKNOWLEDGE YOUR SUFFERING
Be mindful of your default patterns, habitual behaviours and thoughts. Recognising, 'Ah these are my negative thoughts again' helps break the cycle of believing them.

OFFER KINDNESS TO YOURSELF
Let go of self-criticism, and offer yourself the sort of kindness you would give to others if they were struggling. Ask 'What do I really need right now?'

WIDEN YOUR PERSPECTIVE
When we struggle we feel alone, resentful, inward looking. Seeing ourselves as part of this flawed, imperfect, complex human race can be comforting.

LIBERATE YOURSELF FROM EXTERNAL VALIDATION
Let go of the craving for approval and validation – try not to align your future inner happiness with how you are perceived by others.

HAVE COURAGE AND RELINQUISH SELF-JUDGEMENT
Self-compassion demands courage to do hard things. You may have reacted a certain way in the past; allow yourself the possibility of going down a different path.

> **"WE RESERVE OUR UNDERSTANDING FOR OTHERS. WE CONSIDER SELF-NURTURING AS INDULGENT"**

© Getty Images / Rudzhan Nagiev

WHY IT'S GOOD TO Cry

Sometimes a proper blub is the best thing we can do to improve our mood

WORDS DEBRA WATERS

If you've ever found yourself crying at an advert or a scene in a soap opera, for example, you may have been accused of being a tad too emotional. But we cry for a reason and, as the saying goes, it's better out than in. In fact, it can do us the world of good.

Surprisingly, scientists don't really know what goes on inside us when we cry. "We know that crying is a parasympathetic reaction [the parasympathetic nervous system is our rest-and-digest function], but we're not yet certain whether this activity is the cause or the result of the crying," says clinical psychologist Professor Ad Vingerhoets. Here's what we do know about crying's ability to help and heal...

The power of tears

Aside from the fact that crying makes us feel better – one study found that 50% of participants reported an improvement in their mood after shedding tears – people are more likely to reach out to us, and even like us more, if they see us upset.

"It stimulates empathy in others, so that they're more willing to provide support and comfort," says Professor Vingerhoets. "To put it differently, tears connect." Research reveals that tearful people are seen as warmer, nicer, more reliable and honest. "They are the kind of people we want as friends, neighbours and colleagues," he says. "We consider them as fit for 'reliable' professions such as doctor, teacher and police officer."

Release the pressure

Although one in ten people will feel worse after crying, and some will get a headache or sore eyes, many of us benefit from the experience.

"Crying is our body's way of releasing emotion – a feeling, a pressure, something you've been holding in," explains psychotherapist Anna Mathur, author of *Know Your Worth* (£14.99/$18.50, Waterstones). "When we hold a lot of emotions, we can become like a pressure cooker, until our body finds a way to let things go. You might feel tempted to rationalise tears when they flow over something seemingly insignificant, but try to respect this feeling until it passes."

It helps to heal

Have you noticed how, after crying, you feel calmer and more clear headed? Or that shedding a few tears after stubbing your toe makes the pain go away more quickly? This is because of your body's response to crying. "By letting tears go, you are welcoming a release of happy hormones – endorphins and oxytocin – which can induce anti-stress-like effects, such as a reduction of blood pressure and cortisol levels," says Anna. "These endorphins also interact with receptors in your brain, which can even reduce your perception of pain."

TAKING CONTROL

IF IT'S NOT A GOOD TIME TO CRY...

It's not unusual for us to feel embarrassed when we cry. "If we're afraid that observers don't consider crying an appropriate reaction to a situation, we experience distress," says Professor Vingerhoets.

- Try not to panic – instead, focus on breathing in through your nose, holding for two seconds, then breathing out slowly through pursed lips. This will steady your breath and help you regain control.
- Touching the roof of your mouth with your tongue or pinching yourself may also curb crying.

DON'T FEEL BETTER?

If you're crying more than feels cathartic, or your emotions feel overwhelming for more than two weeks, see your doctor, says Anna. Persistent tearfulness can be a sign of depression or anxiety.

REDISCOVER YOUR *Optimism*

Worn out by worrying and dwelling on the negative? It's time to turn things around

WORDS EVA GIZOWSKA

It can be hard not to let negativity seep in to your day, especially during stressful periods of life. A dose of optimism not only makes you feel better, but it's also good for your physical and emotional health – even if initially you need to force yourself to feel more positive. "An optimistic person is always looking for the best in any situation and expecting good things to happen," says Kimberly Reed, author of *Optimists Always Win* (£10.95, Health Communications Inc.). "Even if something negative happens, such as the loss of a job, an optimist sees the silver lining. For example, the chance to pursue a more fulfilling career or hobby, or take a much-needed break. Optimists believe their actions result in positive outcomes, that they are responsible for their own happiness, and that they can expect more good things in the future."

If you're an optimist you try to look for good in every situation. "An optimist views adverse events (such as your car being broken into, redundancy and so on) as a result of something outside of themselves," explains Kimberly. "But, even if it's something that happened as a result of an action they took, an optimist will always try to see what they can learn from the experience. They think of an unfortunate event as a temporary setback – not a permanent way of life. Even if something awful happens, a positive thinker believes good things will come again."

"Optimists look on the bright side," reveals psychologist Dr Sandra Wheatley (potentpsychology.com). "They emanate a hopeful positivity. But, being optimistic doesn't mean you go into denial and pretend everything is fine when it's not. It's a frame of mind where you hope for the best but prepare for the worst."

She adds that an optimist can look at a situation squarely in the eye and plan what to do if things go wrong. "By having a contingency plan, this makes it easier to turn things around before there's a huge problem."

Get the optimistic mindset

"Optimists tend to share several positive characteristics that can lead to greater happiness and promote good health," says Kimberly. An optimist:

Thinks about, reflects on and emphasises the good things in life

Tries not to waste time and energy on complaining when something goes wrong, but focuses on what they do to change or learn from a situation

Feels that nothing can hold them back from achieving success and reaching their goals

Sees challenges and obstacles as opportunities to learn

Feels gratitude for the good bits – even in a negative situation

Has a positive attitude towards themselves and others

Is tenacious and carries on when the going gets tough

Doesn't let one bad experience colour their expectations of the future

Accepts responsibility for mistakes but doesn't dwell on them

Is always looking for ways to make the most of any opportunities that come their way

There's a common assumption that optimism is the same as happiness, but that's not the case. "While optimism can lead to greater happiness, it's actually to do with how you view the world," says Dr Wheatley. "Optimists experience difficulties »

> "AN OPTIMIST THINKS OF AN UNFORTUNATE EVENT AS A TEMPORARY SETBACK RATHER THAN A PERMANENT WAY OF LIFE"

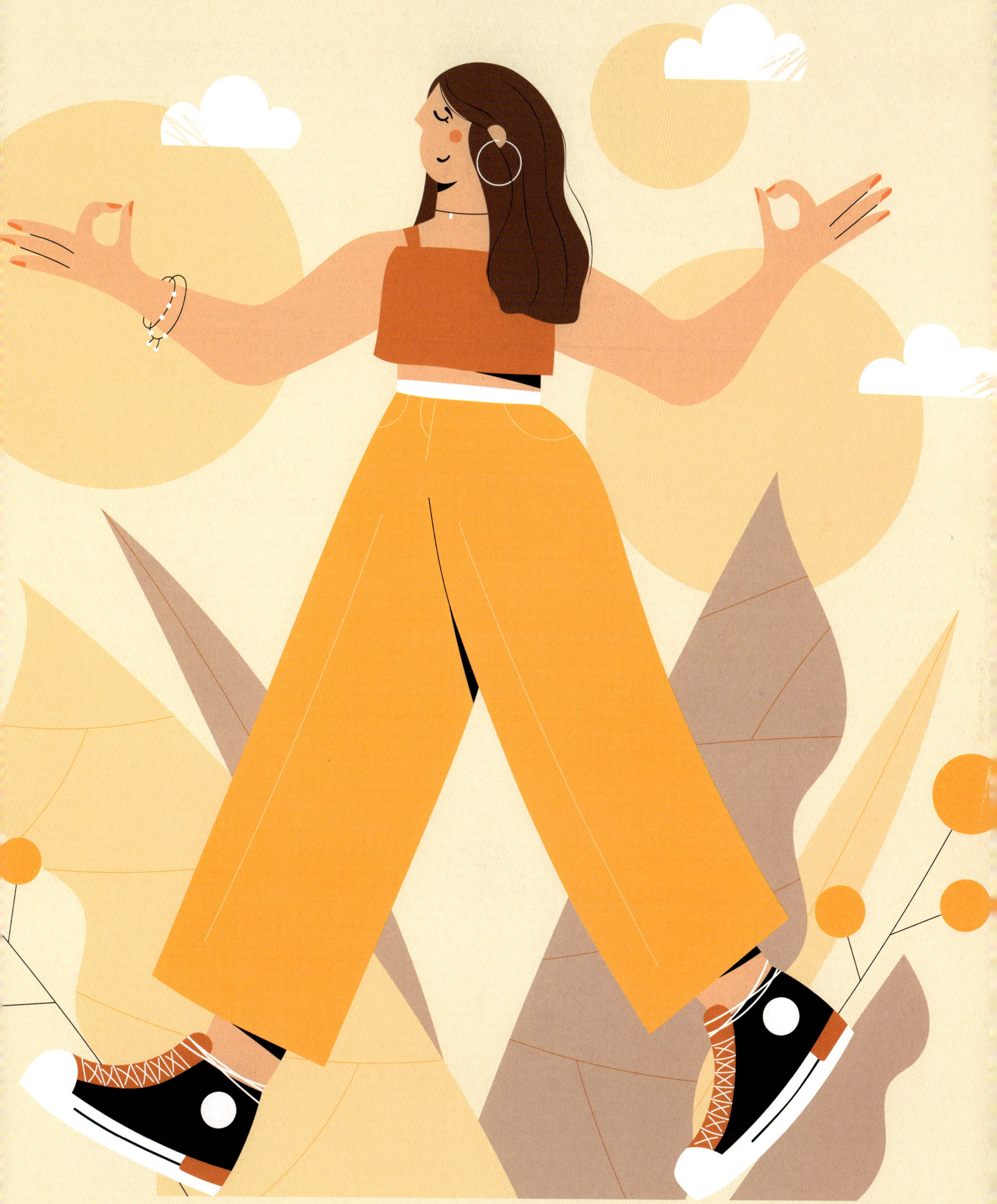

> "OPTIMISTS HAVE MORE EFFECTIVE COPING STRATEGIES"

and problems like anyone else. To be an optimist doesn't protect you from feeling negative emotions. If something bad happens, you still feel the pain, upset, grief, betrayal or disappointment. It's just that an optimistic mindset helps you cope better."

In a recent Indian study* it was shown that optimists tend to have more effective coping strategies, which helps them to feel less stressed. Pessimists, on the other hand, have a tendency to dwell on stressful feelings, which can make them feel worse.

So, what makes some people more optimistic than others? "Some people are just born naturally optimistic, it's part of their genetic make-up," explains Dr Wheatley. "But your upbringing also has an impact. If you grew up in an environment where there was a focus on the positive, the likelihood is that this would have had an effect on your own attitude to life." Likewise, research shows that if you had a parent who was pessimistic or depressed, you're far more likely to have a pessimistic outlook on life as an adult. But, ultimately, optimism is a choice, and anyone can acquire a more optimistic mindset that will help you to face life's challenges and feel confident that you can expect positive things to happen in the future.

HEALTH BENEFITS OF BEING AN OPTIMIST

Latest research shows that optimism is associated with a number of physical and psychological benefits.

It's good for your heart
In a recent US review of 15 studies that looked at 200,000 people** it was shown that optimists had a 35% lower risk of developing heart disease and a 14% reduced incidence of early death.

It lowers your stress hormones
A study at Concordia University, Canada, asked participants to measure their daily stress levels. Optimists were found to have lower levels of stress hormones (such as cortisol). Pessimists, who were shown to go into 'fight or flight' mode more frequently, triggered by negative thinking that exacerbated stress, had higher stress hormones. When cortisol remains constantly elevated, this can lead to health problems.

You'll recover better from illness
A positive mindset can help you to cope better with disease and recover better. In a recent study*** it was shown that optimists had less inflammation and recovered more quickly after a stroke than those who had a more negative outlook. In another study, published in the Journal of Psychosomatic Research in 2014, it was shown that optimism is associated with reduced pain and symptoms after heart surgery.

You're more likely to live longer
Optimists are more likely to live a longer life – 11-15% longer – and have a greater chance of reaching 85 years of age, compared to those who have a more pessimistic disposition. These are the findings of a study by the Boston University School of Medicine in 2019 that followed nearly 70,000 women and 1,500 men over a timespan of 10 to 30 years.

It can help you to manage pain
According to a recent review, optimists who expect positive outcomes are better able to cope with and manage pain. It seems that a positive attitude can help to reduce the perception of pain. Whereas feeling negative, pessimistic and depressed appears to have a more adverse effect on someone's experience of pain; for example, they find it more difficult to manage.

It's an antidote to depression and makes you more resilient to stress
Another study, in the Natural Medicine Journal in 2017, showed that people who are optimistic consider themselves as inherently protected (not vulnerable) and think about the world as a generally good place. They tend to be happier, have a lower chance of facing depression, and manage stress more effectively. They're more likely to practise healthy habits such as exercising, following a healthy diet and not smoking. And they are more likely to seek help if they need it than a pessimist would.

7 WAYS TO BE MORE OPTIMISTIC

1. RECOGNISE OPTIMISM IS A CHOICE YOU CAN MAKE EVERY DAY

"This doesn't mean you feel positive all the time; it's having the confidence to know you can cope with whatever life throws your way," says Dr Wheatley. "It means acknowledging the negative, while making a conscious effort to think optimistically. For example, it can be as simple as choosing to smile when you feel glum. It's your choice to feel down, or to do something positive to take your mind in a different direction. You can't control everything, but if there's one thing you can control, it's what you think."

2. BE MINDFUL OF NEGATIVE THINKING

Next time you catch yourself having a negative thought, swap it for a positive one. "This might take some practice but after a while it will start to feel more natural," says Dr Wheatley. "If you've had a bad day, tell yourself, 'Tomorrow will be better' and plan on what you can do to make it that way. Or, if you know you've got a Zoom meeting with a tricky client, rather than approaching it with dread, prepare for the challenge and do your best, but afterwards let it go."

3. PRACTISE GRATITUDE

"Gratitude allows you to redirect your focus," says Kimberly. "When you feel grateful, your mind shifts your focus from what you should have more of, to what's good in your life right now. Practising gratitude is a process of trying your best to see and be thankful for the positives in your life, even in the midst of a difficult situation."

4. TURN OFF THE NEWS

How often do you wake up in a perfectly good mood, only to turn on the news and you end up feeling angry, disappointed, fed up, fearful or depressed with everything that's going on in the world? "Limit yourself to anything that makes you feel bad," says Dr Wheatley. "If that includes watching the news, then watch something uplifting instead and let in the information that supports you."

5. BE MINDFUL OF WHO YOU SPEND TIME WITH

"When you surround yourself with people who make you feel happy and relaxed, this automatically makes you feel more positive," explains Dr Wheatley. "That doesn't mean you can't share problems, or have off days, it's just that if you've got a good circle of friends, who uplift and inspire you, it's easier to feel optimistic." She adds that negativity often comes from spending too much time on your own and overthinking things. "That's why it's important to make time for your friends – even if it's just to meet for a walk or talk on the phone."

6. GET ACTIVE

"Rather than complaining, moaning and feeling sorry for yourself, take a walk, go for a bike ride, or hit the gym," says Kimberly. "The idea is to get your body moving. Physical activity releases endorphins and you're less likely to feel pessimistic with these feel-good neurochemicals circulating in your body. If you don't know where to start, download a fitness app."

7. REFRAME PAST SETBACKS

If you find your mind wandering to a past disappointment, such as a job or relationship that didn't work out, think of all the details you can remember, trying to be as objective as you can. "In what way would you have wanted the situation to turn out better? Now reframe the situation by letting go of what you wanted to happen and write a paragraph about what good came out of it," says Kimberly. Perhaps you got a better job, or made a new circle of friends.

SURVIVAL OF THE KINDEST

Survival
OF THE
KINDEST

In a dog-eat-dog world where animals battle daily for survival, how did kindness ever evolve? What stops selfishness from taking over? And what are the benefits of being kind?

WORDS LAURA MEARS

Nature is violent. In a world where only the fittest survive, animals must engage in deadly battles to pass their selfish genes to the next generation. But, there's a wrinkle in this tale of teeth and claws. Sometimes, it's the kindest that survive.

Biologically speaking, our primary goal as animals is to maximise our evolutionary fitness – our chances of passing on our genes to the next generation. And, in theory, every act of kindness comes at a cost. By putting the needs of others above our own, we reduce our evolutionary 'fitness' and increase theirs.

Imagine a society where everyone is kind – if you do something nice for someone, they'll do something nice for you. You sacrifice some of your evolutionary fitness for them, but they pay you back. The evolutionary scales are balanced. What happens if someone cheats the system? You do something nice for them, but they do nothing kind in return. They improve their

> **"KINDNESS MAKES US FEEL GOOD, EVEN WHEN NO ONE IS LOOKING"**

own chances of success and leave you in the dust. If evolution were governed by a simple balance sheet that pitted the selfish against the selfless, kindness would rapidly disappear. Luckily, it's not that simple.

Better together
The truth is, the evolutionary scales don't operate on a purely individual basis. Families that are kind to each other have an evolutionary advantage. If your goal is to pass your genetic code on to the next generation, being kind to your sister, who shares your genes, helps to outweigh your own evolutionary sacrifice. Unrelated groups that are kind to each other also fare better. A group of individuals who work together can easily outcompete a group of individuals who care only for themselves. And, when we cooperate, something magical happens – we become more than the sum of our parts.

Human civilisation is built on kindness among complete strangers. We work together in groups to share favours on a scale completely unmatched in the animal kingdom. We divide tasks among individuals to achieve more than any one of us ever could alone. We're kind to strangers, not because we want something from them as an individual, but because we all benefit from the kindness of society as a whole.

Being kind is so important to our survival that it's become hard-wired. We might not repay every act of kindness immediately, but we feel guilt and shame when we don't treat others well. When we see someone suffering, we feel their pain. When we stop to help, we're rewarded with a rush of endorphins. Kindness makes us feel good, even when no one is looking, and this is the secret to humanity's success.

You get what you give
When it comes to kindness, you get back almost as much as you put in, with every altruistic action making you happier and healthier than before. Pure kindness comes from a place of selflessness. But whether you do a favour because you want something in return, or out of the goodness of your heart, you can't help but reap the rewards. Every act of kindness you perform has subtle effects on your physiology. Your heart rate slows down, feel-good chemicals flood your system, and your outlook on the world starts to change. Being kind is more than just a gift to those around you – it changes your internal chemistry, making you happier and healthier from the inside out.

Load up on happy hormones
Every act of giving releases feel-good chemicals that change your physiology for the better. Oxytocin is the body's most powerful chemical signal of social connection. Produced by the brain, it travels through the bloodstream and floods every corner of the body. It has antidepressant-like effects, boosting feelings of empathy, increasing trust, suppressing fear, and making us more generous. It also dampens the release of the stress hormone, cortisol, and even seems to decrease inflammation, helping wounds to heal faster.

Heal your neighbour
Some acts of kindness have a health benefit for others, as well as for yourself. When you put your hand on someone's shoulder and gently stroke their forearm, you are doing something called 'affective touch'. This soothing type of physical kindness activates specific nerve fibres that respond only to gentle stroking. These nerve fibres trigger a release of opiates, the body's natural morphine, relieving both physical and emotional pain. Slow touches from people we trust tell us that we're safe, and it's going to be okay.

Reduce everyday stress
Helping others doesn't make hard days harder. In fact, on stressful days, making the effort can make all the difference. Research shows that even the tiniest acts of kindness can help to keep negative emotions at bay. Try something small, like holding open a door for someone.

Start a happiness spiral
Research shows that counting kindnesses is a simple way to get more happiness out of your day. Just bringing attention to kindness in your life can instantly improve your mood. Then, a little magic starts to happen. When we feel happy, we are more likely to be kind. And, when we are kind, we are more likely to have positive social interactions. This strengthens our social connections, which makes us happy, and the upward cycle continues.

Feel more connected
Comparing yourself to others can lead to feelings of disconnection, but you can counteract this with kindness. Research shows that wishing others well, even just in your head, can increase your sense of connection. Thoughts of 'loving kindness' lower anxiety and boost happiness. »

ANIMAL INSTINCTS

Cases of animals performing selfless acts suggest that the trait of kindness isn't exclusive to humans. A famous example took place in the summer of 1996, when a three-year-old boy slid over the railings at Brookfield Zoo, Illinois, tumbling into a gorilla enclosure. The fall broke his arm and knocked him unconscious. But in an incredible act of animal kindness, eight-year-old Binti Jua came to his aid. The 150-pound gorilla looped her arm around the boy's waist and lifted him to safety. She positioned herself between the infant and six other adult gorillas, cradled him gently, and delivered him to paramedics waiting at the door to her enclosure.

Buffer a low mood
We often judge ourselves more harshly than we judge others, amplifying feelings of isolation, loneliness and rejection. Replacing that judgement with self-care and self-compassion is sometimes all it takes to lift a low mood. Remember to be kind to yourself, too.

Relax and live longer
Being kind and sharing your time for the benefit of others seems to reduce your risk of dying. The reasons for this aren't completely clear, but one explanation is happiness: positive emotions make you healthier. Kindness makes people feel more connected, and this affects the vagus nerve, which controls the 'rest' modes of the heart, lungs and guts. The vagus nerve also opposes the 'fight or flight' response. Building social connections can help the vagus nerve to work better, taking the body out of threat mode and back into rest mode.

Help a whole community
Receiving an act of kindness makes people more likely to perform an act of kindness themselves, triggering a chain reaction. Your kindness not only improves your own health, but the health of everyone who chooses to pass that kindness on.

Get high on helping
Kindness isn't always selfless, and the brain's reward pathway knows it. It lights up when we do something kind, because it knows that when we help someone else, they often return the favour. But kindness can also be its own reward. Even when we practise pure altruism, with no expectation of receiving anything in return, we still get that same rush of dopamine. The feel-good chemical is a reward in itself, a 'helper's high', and the sensation can be addictive.

Heal a broken heart
The hormone surge generated by random acts of kindness has the power to protect your heart. Oxytocin acts on the heart and blood vessels, lowering blood pressure, slowing the heart rate, and reducing inflammation. It might also be able to help a broken heart to heal.

Relieve physical pain
According to brain-scan research, being kind can numb physical pain. The parts of the brain involved in pain-processing seem to dial down their activity when we act altruistically. In the study, participants received small electric shocks while researchers monitored their brains. Not only did the volunteers feel less pain when they had done something kind for someone else, but the effect also scaled according to how kind they felt they had been. The kinder they were, the less it hurt. ∎

> "EVEN THE TINIEST ACTS OF KINDNESS CAN HELP TO KEEP NEGATIVE EMOTIONS AT BAY"

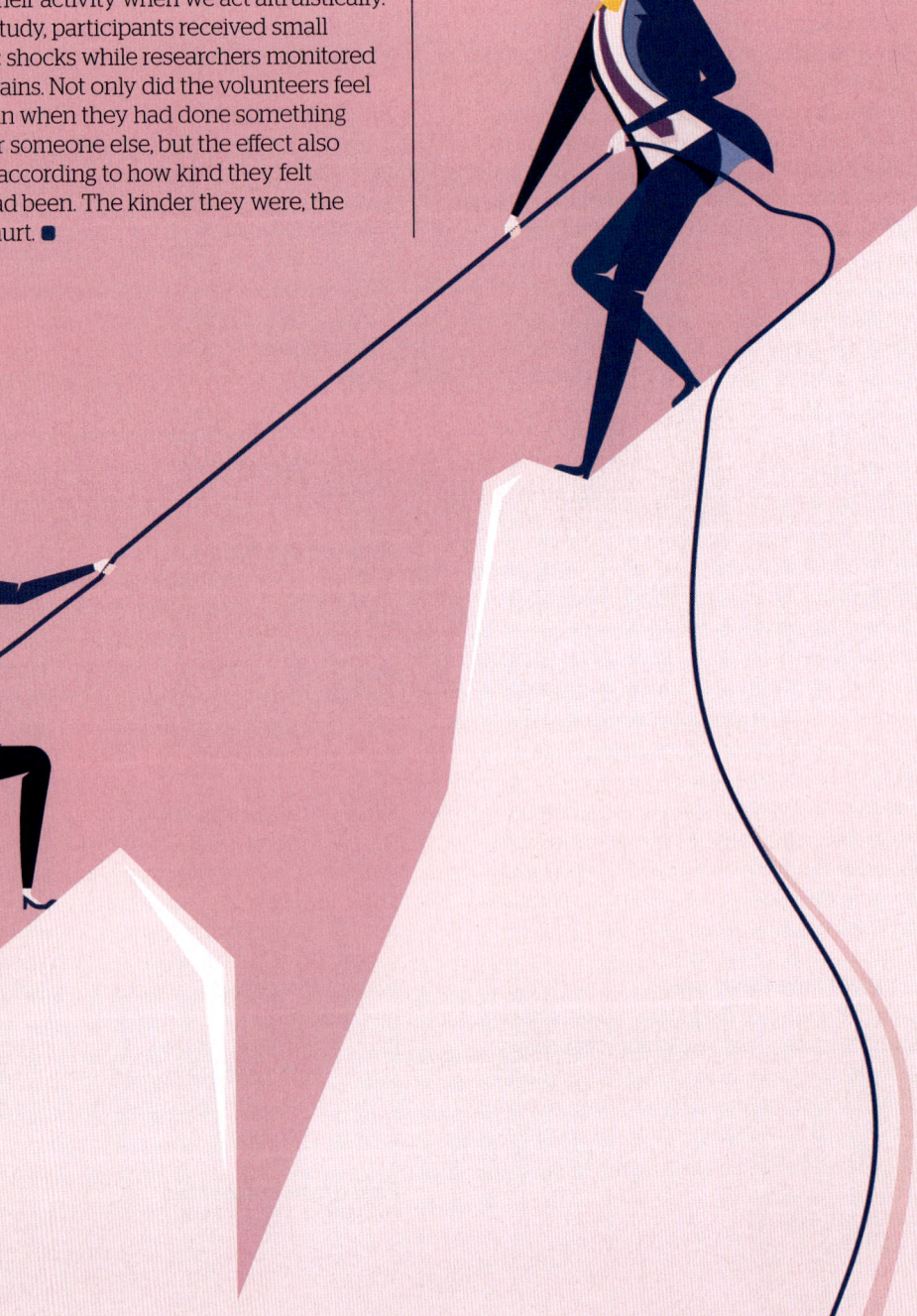

ON SALE NOW!

Track your feelings and identify patterns

Build a complete picture of the mood influences in your life – record information on your sleep, diet, physical health, mental health and much more. Look at how these factors affect how you feel in order to make small changes to improve your moods.

Ordering is easy. Go online at:

WWW.MAGAZINESDIRECT.COM

Or get it from selected supermarkets & newsagents

GRATITUDE & WELLBEING

Gratitude & Wellbeing

The simple act of focusing on the positives in your life can have a huge impact on your physical and mental wellbeing

WORDS JULIE BASSETT

Sometimes life has a habit of getting you down. There's no need to feel bad – it happens to us all from time to time. The everyday routine can become mundane, and we can feel so busy that time seems to fly by without anything really seeming to happen. It can be hard to look at the positives in your life, but there are real benefits, both physical and mental, if you take the time to harness the power of gratitude.

Recognising things and people in your life that you're grateful for can have a huge impact on your wellbeing. "Being grateful for people, things and situations in our lives can create a balanced view in our mindset and lead us to experience the abundance in our lives, rather than feeling closed, deprived and constantly striving to better our lives," explains clinical psychologist Dr Sarah Maynard (www.wildandpreciousminds.com). "Learning to feel grateful shows us what there is to appreciate and be thankful for in our lives right now, and can create a sense of contentment and fulfilment, without actually changing anything. This in turn can be something that lowers our stress levels and affects us physically."

This feeling of gratefulness can impact different areas in your life. For example, instead of constantly focusing on what you don't like about your body, remind yourself what it can do from a non-aesthetic perspective. You might be grateful to it for enabling you to walk along the beach, bend down to pick up a child, or take part in an exercise class. By turning your attention to these positives, you are far more likely to feel motivated to look after your body through exercise, healthy eating and mindfulness.

Barriers to gratitude

It can be difficult to show gratitude in our lives if it's new to us. It's not uncommon to be stuck in a negative mindset, seeing the downside and struggling to embrace the good. So, how can we introduce gratitude into our daily lives? Dr Maynard says: "The best way to develop a gratitude habit is to practise little and often. This helps build the neural pathways in our brain so the habit becomes more automatic. A great exercise is the 'ten-finger gratitude practice' (finding something we are grateful for, for each finger), which stretches our thinking so we realise how much there is around us to be grateful for, both the big stuff and the small stuff."

GRATITUDE & WELLBEING

KEEP A GRATITUDE DIARY

A gratitude diary is a great way of helping you to focus on the things you are grateful for. There is no set format for you to start a diary, though there are some you can buy with handy headers and ideas to prompt your thoughts. All you really need, though, is five minutes a day with a notepad and pen.

You really should try and write in your gratitude diary every day, which helps to establish a good habit. Write down anything good that happens in your day. You could carry it with you and journal something as soon as it happens, or you could make it a regular part of your pre-bedtime routine.

There is no limit to the things you can cover. Did you have a nice walk into work? Write it down. Did you manage a task for the first time? Write it down. It can be big things and small things. A gratitude diary is only for noting down the positives, to build up a resource that you can pull out whenever you feel down so you can look back on all the good things that have happened to you.

If you prefer a more structured approach, you could work to a set format in your gratitude diary. You could list five things that you were grateful for today, one person you were grateful for today, and one personal skill you were grateful for today. This can really help to streamline your thoughts, if that's how you work.

The key thing to remember is that this is purely personal – it is what you are grateful for. What makes you happy is very individual, and your diary is a reflection of that.

Give it a try and see if you can isolate those first ten things that you're grateful for in your life right now. If you find it difficult, you're not alone. Dr Maynard explains that there is a psychological reason why this happens: "The brain is typically able to hold on to negative thoughts (so-called 'velcro thoughts') because it determines that these may be important to our survival, whereas positive thoughts (including areas like gratitude) are so-called 'teflon thoughts' because they more easily slip right out of our minds and off our radar unless they are consciously practised."

There are barriers to overcome to embrace a life of gratitude. Dr Maynard says that when we're in a negative mindset, "it's easy to convince ourselves there is nothing good in our lives worth being grateful for, or anything significant to include." This is limiting our ability to show gratitude and it takes practise to let go of this negativity: "If we buy into this thought, we stay stuck. If we get a bit of distance from this thought and recognise 'this is just a thought', we become free to look for things we are grateful for, regardless of whether such thoughts are present or not."

Start to feel grateful
If you would like to introduce gratitude into your life, Dr Maynard has some tips: "Look around you; there is always something to »

> **"BE THANKFUL FOR WHAT YOU HAVE; YOU'LL END UP HAVING MORE. IF YOU CONCENTRATE ON WHAT YOU DON'T HAVE, YOU WILL NEVER, EVER HAVE ENOUGH"**
>
> – OPRAH WINFREY –

GRATITUDE & WELLBEING

be grateful for. Maybe it's simply the fact we are alive. Anything or anyone that brings pleasure and wonder into your life, be it the blue sky, or your committed partner, can be something to be grateful for."

Once you start consciously seeking things you are grateful for, you suddenly start to realise how much good there is around you. It can be worth starting a gratitude diary (see the box below) to list the things you are grateful for each day.

There are so many benefits to being grateful. Those who practise gratitude daily might experience better sleep - one technique is to run through all of the things you are grateful for or everything that was good about your day just before you go to sleep. This puts you in a positive mindset for a good night's sleep, so you can wake up feeling refreshed and ready to face a new day.

As you practise gratitude daily and start to feel the benefits, pass it on by showing your gratitude towards others. "Demonstrating and voicing gratitude towards others can take them by surprise!" says Dr Maynard. "However, it opens up the opportunity to show others how much we value them, and in turn cultivate a more reciprocal exchange of appreciation towards each other. Being grateful also creates a ripple effect; if someone has been the recipient of gratitude, they may be more likely to pass this on in their interactions with others." Whether it's through writing letters, sending flowers or a verbal expression of appreciation, it's well worth sharing your gratitude.

Make today the first day you consciously show gratitude for the good things and people in your life, and see how it impacts on your wellbeing.

> **"ONCE YOU CONSCIOUSLY SEEK THINGS YOU ARE GRATEFUL FOR, YOU REALISE HOW MUCH GOOD THERE IS AROUND YOU"**

WRITE DOWN ALL THE THINGS YOU ARE GRATEFUL FOR

ON SALE NOW!

Acknowledge life's positives for a happier mindset

This 52-week guide has space for you to record the things that make you feel grateful. With prompts and activities to encourage you to appreciate yourself, your home, friends, family, health and much more, see how quickly your mindset improves.

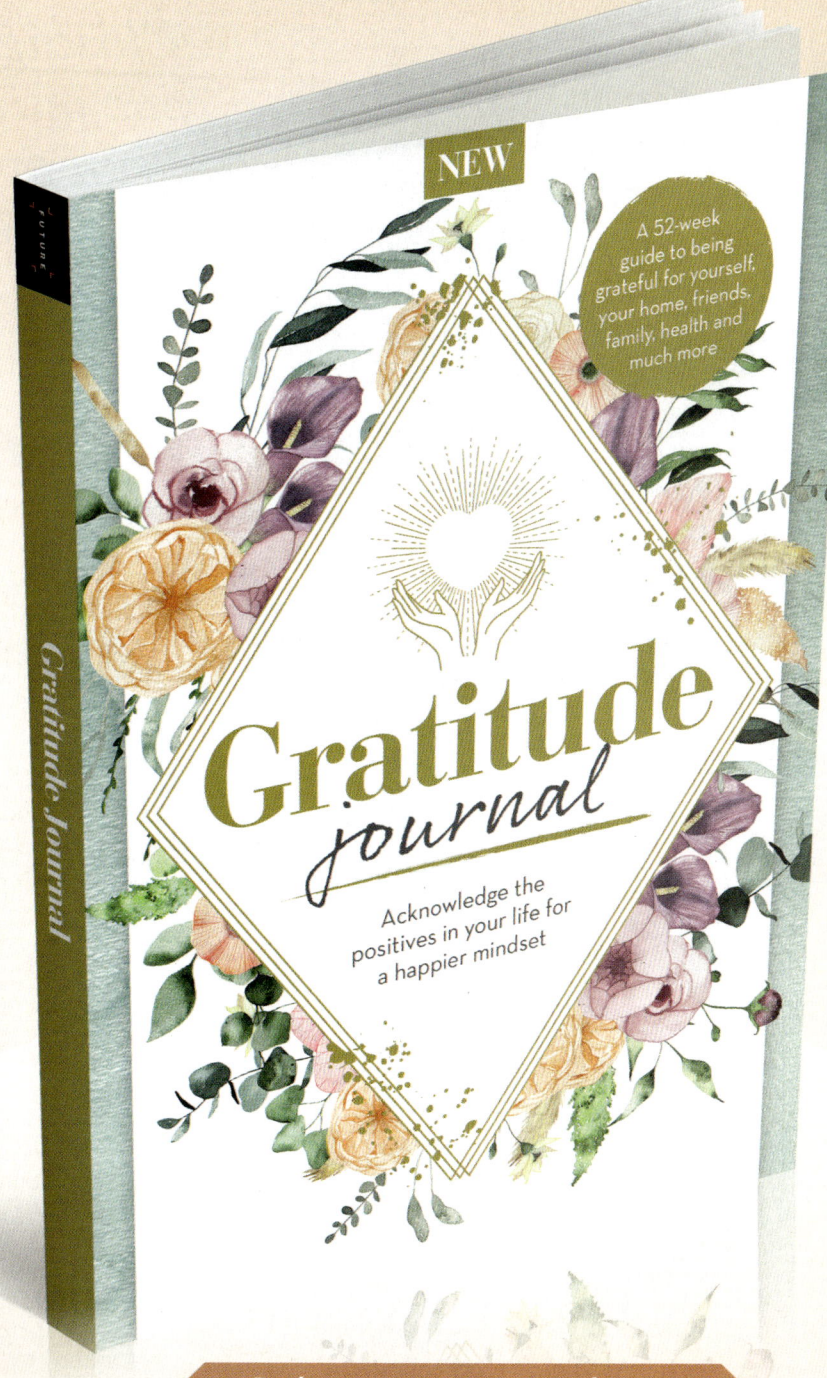

Ordering is easy. Go online at:

WWW.MAGAZINESDIRECT.COM

Or get it from selected supermarkets & newsagents

ACHIEVING FORGIVENESS

Achieving
FORGIVENESS

Closing doors on our painful pasts can open those to the future

WORDS AILSA HARVEY

Forgiving someone isn't an acceptance of the person who has wronged you, and doesn't have to mean that you're now okay with whatever has happened. To forgive someone means you're simply crossing the line between being stuck focused on the past and accepting the present. You no longer want revenge, and the negative feelings that you accumulated in the aftermath are decreasing. Forgiveness is accepting the fact that it did happen, rather than torturing your brain with thoughts of the alternatives. When you are ready to move on and live in the moment, you are ready to forgive.

This sounds much simpler than the reality, especially when circumstances can be complex and range in severity.

LIVE YOURSELF HAPPY

We might think we are ready to move on when our minds have actually just buried the pain, ready for it to resurface later. Human beings are sensitive creatures. Our brains are complex machines, home to a range of emotions, and each one is wired slightly differently. As it rapidly fires signals in response to the events around you, people quickly learn which actions bring them happiness or flood them with dread. Designed to protect your social wellbeing, emotions can keep you away from things that have previously caused heartache, and encourage you to strive for potential rewards.

Some of the most powerful emotions come from betrayal and can have a lasting impact. The strength of the anger, upset and fear that traumatic events can have on us often leaves our minds lacking the trust it may have once held in an individual. Knowing that someone has been the cause of the pain that is affecting our daily life can leave our thoughts of them tinted with resentment. So when should we try to let go of this blame? How can we - and why should we - learn to leave the past behind us?

The truth is there's no quick fix, and beginning the act of forgiveness can't be forced. You might be the type of person who will firmly wedge a barrier between you and an old friend for that one time they let your secret slip, or you may be able to forgive a stranger who has committed a despicable crime. Could you ever forgive someone who had taken the life of someone you love? For some people, it's the only option if they are to move on. It's a process that victims of crime are regularly offered through the criminal justice system. Bringing the victim and the offender face to face can give closure to those who beforehand felt only resentment.

Readiness to forgive varies based on the mindset of the victim and the status of the original relationship. Forgiving a serious and personal crime usually takes more time, as it presents sensitive consequences. However, for smaller acts of offence, we are less likely to need to forgive a stranger. As the person isn't previously known to us, the event seems less personal and can be quickly forgotten, but it's more likely to play on the mind when it involves someone we have collected data on. Your brain knows your best friend well, but this added bit of information taints your overall view of them. To return to the feelings you previously held, you need to forgive and erase this data anomaly.

Coming from someone who was so highly regarded can make betrayals more painful. How could they have done this? Are they the person you originally thought they were? For some, the closer the person is, and the more serious their offence, the harder it can be to forgive the intent behind it. For others, though, this close bond is what helps them

HOW TO FORGIVE

If you have found it challenging to forgive those who mistreated you in the past, that doesn't mean you can't train yourself to forgive. Psychologists often work with those desperate to leave their painful pasts behind them and have discovered that those who struggled beforehand were able to achieve forgiveness with some guidance. One of the main factors standing in the way of this closure was overthinking. When the trauma is revisited regularly and in a negative way, this is called rumination. Whether these are angry, sad or anxious ruminations, they can continue to jeopardise mental wellbeing for as long as they persist. By keeping the neural signals for negative emotions firing in the brain, there's not enough space between these thoughts for the forgiving process to develop. The best way to enable forgiveness is to try to empathise with the perpetrator, as hard as it may seem. Only when you try to understand the true reasons and stop demonising the 'enemy' can you begin to get clarity and attempt acceptance.

Negative emotions often can't be controlled easily, so when they do occur, acknowledging your feelings is the best step to take. Actively telling yourself 'I feel angry' will force you to remain aware of your feelings in order to learn from them. Almost like you're an outsider witnessing your thoughts, your psychological distancing will enable you to eventually regain some power over your mind.

forgive. Rather than focusing on the betrayal, these people are more likely to dwell on the positive aspects of that person. In a romantic relationship, the victim might be inclined to forgive their long-term partner as they think they have more to lose if they don't attempt to forgive. Those who have experienced a betrayal early on in a relationship might be less willing to mend their connection.

Studies analysing the reasons behind people's reluctance to forgive show that most of the time they are avoiding coming across as weak. This is a common misconception. It might feel like you are backing down from your corner during what, in your head, is a fight for justice, but in actuality forgiving someone takes much more power. Finding the mental strength to prevent the disloyalty from taking over your thoughts also empowers your mental health. Not only have you fought the challenge they presented, but you have fought your own misplaced pride.

It's also crucial to acknowledge that even though there are professional psychologists and useful methods available to help you catalyse the process of forgiveness, two people's brains won't work identically in the same scenario. For example, those with smaller insular cortices have been found to be more likely to be forgiving. This is part of the brain that is also responsible for providing feelings of disgust, indicating that those with a tendency of being easily offended may also struggle to forgive. If you find that forgiveness doesn't seem to come naturally to you and it's starting to impact your quality of life, there are mental health professionals who can advise you of the best steps to take. It's a process that takes time, but this time can be essential for healing. When your brain completes this process, the energy it once used to cause pain can now be utilised to keep moving past, through and most importantly forward.

> "HOW CAN WE AND WHY SHOULD WE LEARN TO LEAVE THE PAST BEHIND US?"

Learning TO TRUST

Trust is a powerful emotion that builds relationships and connections, but our lived experiences feed into our ability to trust

WORDS JULIE BASSETT

Trust is a key part of good relationships and friendships, yet it doesn't come as easily to some of us as it does to others. It's hard to define what trust is. Sure, there is the dictionary definition – 'a firm belief in the reliability, truth or ability of someone or something' – but real trust is far less tangible than that. Our ability to trust in the people around us is influenced by our experiences, our past, our instincts and our personality.

Trust is something that is at the heart of our daily life in many ways. We have to put our trust in people at work, when commuting, for our medical health and so on. Every time you order a taxi, you're putting your trust in the driver to get you safely from A to B. When you hire someone to deliver a service (a tradesperson, for example, or a babysitter), you have to trust that they will do a good job. When you have a confidential business conversation with a new client, you need to trust that they won't pass knowledge on. You need to have trust in medical professionals, government bodies and employers to have your best interests at heart. Trust is a thread that runs through all our connections, from the closest relationships to people we meet only fleetingly. When trust is broken, it can be hard to restore, and it can influence how we trust in the future.

When it comes to meeting people for the first time, we unknowingly take a lot of cues from the environment around us, as well as the behaviour and appearance of the person we're meeting. Not only that, cultural and societal influences have a large part to play in our ability to trust. Think back to your childhood: how often were you told not to speak to strangers? How many stories have you read over the years where terrible things have happened to victims at the hands of people they trusted? How many times have you heard of people falling for scam emails or phone calls because they trusted what they were told? Everything we have heard, seen and experienced in our life feeds into our ability to trust people now. If you've had your heart broken, you may find it hard to trust a new partner. If a friend spills your secrets, you won't be able to trust them in the future. If you're passed over at work for a promotion you were promised, you might not be able to trust your boss is looking out for you. If you're misdiagnosed by a medical professional, you may always distrust doctors. There are hundreds of scenarios throughout our lives that contribute to the way we trust. The deepest trust is developed over time, whether that's with our partners, our family or our oldest friends. Those people who we feel comfortable around, share our secrets and fears with, and feel safe among. But we need to be able to build trust with new people too.

Trust is complex. Without knowing it, we subconsciously apply all of these learnings and experiences to situations in which we need to trust someone. Often this manifests itself as instinct; when we meet someone new, we get a 'feeling' about whether we can trust them or not. We also need to trust our own instincts; if we've been burned once by someone we put trust into, we may then not trust ourselves to not make the same mistakes again and question our ability to read situations or people.

How much these past experiences influence future trust varies hugely from person to person, depending on our personalities. Some people can dissociate past experiences from future experiences - they understand that because one person treated them in a particular way, doesn't mean that another person will be the same. Others find it harder to let go and project past trauma into present situations. Some people are naturally more cynical about the world around them; some are incredibly open and accepting for new possibilities. Trust is more than a feeling;

5 WAYS TO BUILD TRUST

If you want to develop trust in a new relationship or friendship, try these top tips.

LISTEN
When someone you're with is talking, listen to them properly and intently. Trust is a two-way connection and as they open up to you, you'll feel more confident about opening up in return.

COMMUNICATE YOUR WORRIES
If you find it hard to trust due to a specific past experience, then don't be afraid to explain this, and that you're trying to learn to trust again. Honesty breeds trust.

TAKE YOUR TIME
Don't rush into anything. Take a little time to build a new relationship and the trust that comes with it, and stick to your boundaries.

DON'T ASSUME
Set aside your doubts for a period of time; it can be easy to fall into a trap thinking that a person is going to let you down in some way that you've experienced before, but you need to give each fresh connection a chance to flourish (or not) on its own terms.

TAKE A RISK
Be bold! Put yourself into a situation where you need to put a little trust into the other person. Book an activity to do together, or arrange to go somewhere new, putting you both outside of your comfort zone a little and therefore needing to have faith in each other.

it's an emotion, and like any emotion it can be hard to control or question.

There is also, potentially, a chemical element to trust. The working theory is that trust can be linked to oxytocin, which we already know plays a key role in social bonding and love. One study* suggests that oxytocin plays a role in a person's willingness to accept social risks - choosing to trust someone does require taking a risk.

Whether you're someone who trusts too easily, or someone who is very distrustful, there are ways that you can manage to develop a healthy level of trust. It starts with being able to set your own boundaries and values, rather than being influenced by society, family or belief. Focus on what you believe in, what values you hold close to your heart and who you are. This will help you to live your life in a way that's true to you as a person, and these new experiences will then feed into your instincts and trust, helping you build new relationships. When you meet people, explore your feelings and gut instinct over whether you trust them - question why you feel that way and what could be feeding into those emotions. Over time, you'll learn to trust your instincts, finding a balance between being able to trust and being open to new relationships, and protecting your boundaries and wellbeing.

If your inability to trust comes from a significant past trauma, you may need professional help to move forward. Talking to someone through therapy, for example, can help you to face your experiences and give you the support you need to move forward, helping you to learn to trust again.

> " OUR ABILITY TO TRUST IS INFLUENCED BY OUR EXPERIENCES "

*Kosfeld, M., Heinrichs, M., Zak, P. et al. Oxytocin increases trust in humans. Nature 435, 673–676 (2005)

# Regrets *are* GOOD FOR YOU

Stuck in a rut of wishing you'd done things differently? It's hard to break free, but processing regrets can help us move forward

REGRETS ARE GOOD FOR YOU

WORDS CLARE BOWIE

Ever wish you'd left the house earlier, reworded that email or stopped short of being cajoled into a full head of highlights? We all have regrets, big and small, and the good news is that we should be giving ourselves permission to have them. No more ruminating over what we did or didn't do – the new goal is not to be a victim of the past, and to learn to accept ourselves just as we are.

1 ACKNOWLEDGE REGRETS

Regrets are a common experience and it's unrealistic to believe that life can, or should, be devoid of them. The sorrow over 'fundamental regrets' (relationships, work, health, life choices and so on) can "run deep and feel very intense," says Karin Sieger. The key is to acknowledge their existence and then learn how to manage them. Nobody can sashay through life getting it correct every time, making all the right decisions at exactly the right moments. Of course, there may well be a job or relationship that you still dwell on but, by acknowledging that these feelings exist, you can learn to rationalise their impact by choosing the level of emotional pull they have over you.

DO IT Take back control by giving yourself permission to acknowledge that the regret exists, but detach from the emotional impact you are feeding it with. "Regrets can make us feel stuck and block us from growing and fulfilling our potential," says Sieger. Remind yourself that regrets are human – we all have them.

2 ACCEPT THE PAST

Inflexible thinking can trap us in a cycle of regretting past decisions, according to Windy Dryden. "We blame ourselves for what has happened rather than seeing our behaviour in a wider context and understanding why we took the path we did, based on the information we had at the time." We may have spent years regretting a decision like not going for a new job, deciding not to breastfeed or emigrating to the other side of the world, when the truth is that that decision probably made sense at the time. It's only with hindsight it perhaps falls short of the romantic fixed narrative we had constructed for ourselves; the impossible standards we have set in our personal or professional lives.

DO IT Dryden suggests we try switching the negative conversations in our heads to productive ones. Instead of 'I should have done that', self-berating, try asking the harder questions, 'I wonder why I did/didn't do that?'. The answers will help you to remove your blinkers, accept your past self and open the door to repair.

3 BREAK THE HABIT

Okay, so you've realised that regrets can be persistent and very convincing. Sieger refers to them as "slippery and seductive," because they draw you in and exhaust your emotional reserves. To help you move on and break the cycle of ruminative regret, Dryden suggests the next step is to "neither engage nor try to eliminate them." Try thinking of something you regret, like a conversation with a friend where you gossiped too much. Don't dwell on all the details, fuelling your frustration and shame. Instead, allow the memory to exist but not consume or rule you.

DO IT If you feel the familiar negative thought pattern seeping in, breathe slowly inwards and think to yourself, 'What can I learn from this?'. Remind yourself of Dryden's words: 'I thought it was right at the time I did it. It may have been bad, but I'm not bad'. Breathe deeply, exhale the negative emotion and choose not to re-engage with it.

4 LEARN FROM REGRETS

Regrets represent our conscience and they can motivate us to take corrective action in the future. Pinpoint what it is that makes you feel regretful, and what traps you keep falling into. Perhaps you drink too much, overspend, or speak without thinking first. Aim to tweak your future responses. Making a poor decision does not mean that you are doomed to permanent failure. As Sieger reminds us, "Regrets can turn into the experiences that help you unfold your potential."

DO IT Practise mindful strategies like counting to ten before reacting in triggering situations. Be aware of the impact of your words. Focus on things you can control, like starting a spending diary or monitoring your alcohol intake.

5 LET YOURSELF OFF THE HOOK

Sieger's most powerful message is that we should forgive ourselves and step away from negative thought patterns by "acting on regrets, responsibly and fairly towards others and most of all towards ourselves." Remind yourself that it's never too late and, if handled correctly, many an important life lesson and positive change can grow out of regrets. Candi Williams reiterates this thought process and describes how limiting it is to try to live a life where everything is 'perfect'. She recommends that we focus on living purposefully rather than perfectly, so that we can reach a place where we no longer "magnify flaws and play down strengths."

DO IT Williams advises us to conserve our energy for positivity rather than wasting energy holding on to pain. "Learn to let go of things that hurt you, no longer serve you or make you question your worth." The release you feel will "give you more time and space to focus on things that really matter – things that bring you happiness, joy and self-love."

KARIN SIEGER
Karin is a psychotherapist, writer and podcaster. She specialises in help with transitions, anxiety, grief and life-changing illnesses. karinsieger.com

WINDY DRYDEN
Emeritus professor of psychotherapeutic studies at Goldsmiths University, Windy specialises in single-session and very brief interventions. He's written many books, including *Ten Steps to Positive Living* (Routledge).

CANDI WILLIAMS
Candi is the author of *How to be Perfectly Imperfect* (Summersdale).

> **"REGRETS CAN MOTIVATE US TO TAKE CORRECTIVE ACTION"**

YOU CAN'T *Control* EVERYTHING

…but that is okay, because there is joy and magic to be found when you free your thoughts, says former Buddhist monk Björn Natthiko Lindeblad

YOU CAN'T CONTROL EVERYTHING

WORDS FAITH HILL

A 2020 study revealed that we humans have a staggering 6,200 thoughts per day*. But being able to let go of at least some of these helps us to reduce anxiety and stress, making our lives feel lighter and less complicated.

1. LISTEN TO YOUR INNER WISDOM
Learning to listen to yourself, to your innate voice of inner wisdom or intuition, is a valuable life tool. Björn calls it "the intelligence of the moment" and describes it as a finely honed, quiet compass inside you. Other voices may get in the way of your inner wisdom, such as when you seek advice from others. Your ego has a voice too – "It often drowns out everything else with its noisy demands," says Björn. These extra voices shut off access to your own intelligence.
DO IT Create moments of stillness to allow your inner wisdom to speak up. Choose a quiet room and pick a time when you won't be distracted. Björn advises tracking your breathing to find stillness. Follow each inhale, each exhale and any pauses in between.

2. PRACTISE EMPATHY
You may be annoyed by people's behaviour or have opinions about how they should or shouldn't be, but developing empathy will allow you to let go of unhelpful thoughts. Björn lived closely with many different people and all their quirks throughout his monastic journey. "It's only human to find other people annoying. But it can be an unnecessary drain on your resources," he says. Accepting others, just as they are, makes life easier and relaxes you both. The same goes when you feel accepted, just as you are; you feel welcome, without judgement, and are able to move forward with all of your strengths and talents.
DO IT To build empathy for other people, Björn suggests visualising yourself and everyone around you as pebbles on a beach. "When we get to the beach, we're all rough and jagged pebbles. Then the waves of life roll in. And if we can find it in us to stay there and let the other pebbles on the beach jostle us and rub against us and wear us down, our sharp edges will slowly but surely fade."

3. ACCEPT YOU MAY BE WRONG
It can cause suffering if you hold too tightly to fixed thoughts, beliefs or opinions. They may stop you from moving forward when you want to make a change in your life, or means you don't truly listen to someone else in the middle of a disagreement. Being able to let go of a thought or opinion, even if you believe it to be right, can be liberating.
DO IT A wise senior monk shared a valuable mantra with Björn 20 years ago, which has helped him to let go ever since. The mantra is: 'I may be wrong. I may be wrong. I may be wrong'. The next time you sense a conflict brewing, repeat this mantra to let go of fixed thoughts and to become more open to other ideas.

4. LEAVE ROOM FOR MIRACLES
When you think about the future, your mind might spiral into unhelpful negative thought patterns, especially if you have a tendency to imagine worst-case scenarios. For example, if an investment goes south, you might think you'll never recoup the loss. But just because one unwelcome thing happens, it does not mean another will follow. "Loosening our grip on these types of convictions is a sign of wisdom," says Björn. "Trying to direct and predict everything just makes life hard."
DO IT Leave room for miracles to happen, advises Björn. Don't overpack your diary to ensure you have a little time and space each day to 'just be'. A valuable idea or wondrous thought could come at such a moment.

5. LET GO OF 'SHOULD'
Over time, you develop ideas on how things should be, how tasks should be done, or how people should behave. This mindset reduces your flexibility and narrows the chance of you learning something new.

BJÖRN NATTHIKO LINDEBLAD
Swedish public speaker and meditation teacher Björn Natthiko Lindeblad spent 17 years as a Buddhist monk in Thailand, England and Switzerland. He is the author of *I May Be Wrong: And Other Wisdoms from Life as a Forest Monk* (**Bloomsbury, £16.99 ($19.65)**).

Björn witnessed his own 'should' thoughts when he joined a new monastery, which to him was rather disorganised, where "things weren't done in a proper way."
DO IT Practise Björn's simple hand movement to let go of 'should' thoughts: "Clench your fist really hard and then let it unfold into an open hand. It's a good illustration of how we can let go of things we cling to too hard, like feelings or convictions."

6. BALANCE CONTROL WITH TRUST
The phrase 'trust the universe' holds wisdom – it not only encourages positive thinking, but it also helps you to relinquish control. While Björn says there is a place for control in certain circumstances, such as organising your taxes or choosing childcare, there's value in learning to trust, especially if some aspects of life are outside of your control.
"My guiding star on my journey back to work was trust," says Björn who had to navigate re-entry into 'normal' life and find a job after 17 years as a monk.
DO IT "Trying to control everything makes life lonely, tough, fraught and anxious. Trust life a bit more!" says Björn. Ask yourself if trust or control is best for you in a certain situation – perhaps a balance of both is required. You can plan a holiday, but you may have to trust that you will enjoy it.

> **CREATE MOMENTS OF STILLNESS TO ALLOW YOUR INNER WISDOM TO SPEAK UP**

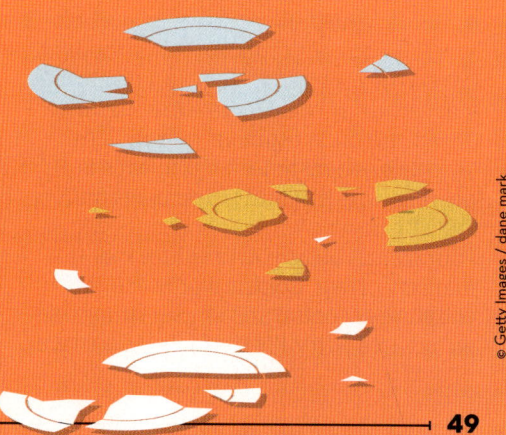

LIVE YOURSELF HAPPY

*Queen's University, Kingston, Canada

WHAT'S *Holding* YOU BACK?

Want to clear away the obstacles that are stopping you from moving forward? The answer is in your hands – here's how

WORDS FAITH HILL

GERRY HUSSEY is a performance psychologist who has worked in the fields of health and performance for 20 years. He shares his personal journey in *Awaken Your Power Within* (£14.99/$18.50, Hachette Books Ireland).

Life can feel like a game of chess – do we make this move or that one? Do we take a risk or play it safe? Sometimes we know what is holding us back from taking a step forward; sometimes we have no idea. Often it is something within us that we have the power to change. Performance psychologist Gerry Hussey gives us six tips for moving past those mental roadblocks.

1 LET GO OF FEAR

Fear – of change, failure, rejection or the unknown – can really hold you back. Yet fear is just a thought, created in your mind. When faced with fear, you can easily overestimate the challenge ahead and underestimate your abilities. You unconsciously set limits to what is possible, which in turn perpetuates the fear.
DO IT Knowing what is – and isn't – within your control helps you to reduce the intensity of fear. "Control that which is within your control and let everything else go," advises Gerry. For example, if you have fear about attending a new social event, remember what you are in control of – for example, what you wear, who you talk to, how much you spend and what time you leave."

2 DON'T GET STUCK IN THE PAST

Each time you think about an event from your past, such as an unresolved trauma or business failure, your brain doesn't know if the event is happening again or if you are just remembering it. It creates the same physical, mental, emotional and physiological responses as the original experience. "This is the state of the 'frozen present'," says Gerry. "As long as you are trapped and imprisoned in it, your thinking and happiness can be no different than they were at the time of trauma."
DO IT The practice of forgiveness is extremely helpful in order to move on. Gerry suggests writing a letter to someone involved to say they are forgiven. Maybe it is even a self-addressed letter, forgiving yourself.

3 LIVE YOUR BEST LIFE

Just like living in the past, worrying about the future can stop you from living your best life now, in the present. "We get caught up in the immediate," says Gerry. "We never reflect and make the required changes to the important things."
DO IT Gerry has a daily mantra that will help to draw you back to the present. Ask yourself, 'What's Important Now?' Use the memorable acronym: 'WIN'.

WHAT'S HOLDING YOU BACK?

4 REALISE YOUR POTENTIAL

Most of your adult beliefs about yourself were developed during the first eight years of your life. These beliefs determine what you do in adulthood. You are capable of achieving the life you want. "Most of us don't take time to ask the bigger questions," reflects Gerry.
DO IT Make a vision board – a collage of images, words and ideas that represents the best version of you and your aspirations for life. Take a large sheet of paper and on it glue pictures and quotes cut from magazines. Put it up in a visible place to inspire you. "Visualisation is a powerful practice to build greater inner resilience, motivation and performance, and helps manifest your goals, dreams and desires," says Gerry.

5 CHANGE THE PERSONALITY 'LABELS' YOU GIVE YOURSELF

Your brain creates labels to help it to organise your thoughts, experiences and memories. Without awareness, you label yourself in an unhelpful manner, such as being uncreative, the quiet type or a bad sleeper. You say phrases such as 'This is just the way I am' or 'That's my personality type'. These self-created labels hold you back. "We dismiss and suppress our true self in the fear that it is not enough and, in doing so, we suppress our dreams, our passions, and we deny ourselves the life we deserve," says Gerry.
DO IT Gerry has three self-enquiry questions to help you break free from self-limiting labels: 'Are these stories and beliefs serving me well? Are they opening my mind and my heart or are they closing them? And are these the stories I want to spend the rest of my life listening to, and living from, or is it time to change the record?' The answer is in your hands.

6 ACCEPT AND LOVE YOURSELF

The starting point of positive transformation is loving yourself for who you are right now. It creates a basis of love and acceptance, rather than one of fear and rejection. From a young age, your brain learns mind-based skills such as comparison with others and self-judgement, which can have a negative effect on your sense of self-worth. However, you also have the ability to learn more helpful, positive skills such as self-compassion and self-love. "It is important we ask ourselves from time to time which part of ourselves we are rejecting and which part of our uniqueness we are strangling," says Gerry.
DO IT Face yourself in the mirror every day. Take a deep breath in and a nice slow exhale out. Look into your eyes and repeat loving affirmations such as 'I am a kind person', 'I honour my caring heart', 'I love and respect myself', 'I am willing to love myself' and 'I am enough'. "The very act of being able to look in the mirror and feel love and pride towards the person you see is the single most transformative step you will ever take," says Gerry.

> "CONTROL THAT WHICH IS WITHIN YOUR CONTROL"

LIVE YOURSELF HAPPY

BEAT THE *Curse* OF COMPARISON

Exhausted trying to keep up with the Joneses? Our experts explain why it's time to stop contrasting your life with others

WORDS ROSE GOODMAN

Feel like you're trying to keep pace with your more adventurous friends? Envious of the colleagues who can afford to retire early while you're still slogging away? Comparing yourself to others is something that we all do – it's human instinct. "Comparison has been hardwired into our DNA for thousands of years," explains therapist Marisa Peer (marisapeer.com). "Previously, in order to stay alive, we learnt how to do things by watching others. It really was the survival of the fittest."

However, fast forward to the current day and pitting ourselves against our peers has become a measuring stick for material worth, personal success and life satisfaction, often breeding low self-esteem, jealousy and depression as a result. One study* found that we tend to overestimate the happiness and success of others, while failing to notice any negatives about their lives – so it comes as no surprise that people can get stuck feeling 'less than' when comparing themselves to others.

The drive to compare

It's not only the younger generation who are in the grip of 'comparison culture'. There's no doubt that social media exposure plays a huge part, thanks to all those manipulated lifestyles and filtered photos, but seeing how we stack up against others isn't just a modern or digital phenomenon. The idea, coined 'social comparison theory', was first developed by social psychologist Leon Festinger in 1954, and it refers to how we evaluate our abilities and attitudes, in comparison with others.

"We compare our personal attributes to those that are accepted within society and use this comparison to identify where we fit in and how valuable we are to it," says positive psychologist Dawn Baxter (beyondthedawnblog.com). So, whether you're checking out your neighbour's new kitchen extension, or scrolling through a friend's birthday party photos, you may find yourself asking questions about the people in your social space and analysing how their situations relate to you. You might think, 'How does she keep her home so beautiful while I struggle to stay on top of housework?' or, 'Why does she look much younger than me when she's actually five years older?'

Coming up short

Everyone compares themselves to others to a certain extent, but some of us are more prone to it. "Lack of confidence, insecurity and anxiety can lead to a greater tendency to make comparisons," says Marisa. "Without a baseline of our own self-worth or success, we can perceive everyone around us to be thriving, and feel frustrated and saddened that we aren't measuring up."

Marisa explains that not getting enough support, praise or approval from those close to us as a child, leads to low self-worth as an adult. The result? Desperately seeking validation in later life, through career or personal achievements – and using others as a

BEAT THE CURSE OF COMPARISON

ARE YOU STUCK IN THE COMPARISON TRAP?

Tick the statements that you agree with to see if comparing yourself to others is having a negative impact on your mental health.

- ☐ If someone achieves something I'm working towards, I feel like a failure.
- ☐ I use Facebook to check up on old friends to see if they're happier and more successful than me.
- ☐ I put on a 'brave face' to others and rarely share my problems.
- ☐ It can feel like everyone is having a better time than me.
- ☐ I mentally measure my body and attractiveness against other women.
- ☐ It makes me feel sad and jealous when others have what I want.
- ☐ My life is very routine and I don't have exciting experiences.

" IT CAN FEED A CYCLE OF ANXIETY AND SELF-LOATHING "

benchmark for this success. The pull of comparison can feel stronger when you're going through difficult times too. For example, if you've recently lost your job, it might feel like everyone else's careers are soaring. "Try to be strict with yourself about this," says Dawn. "Comparing what you've just lost to what others have is self-inflicted emotional torture."

The dark side of comparison
When used in a positive way, comparison can actually help us become better people. "Throughout our lives, we assess where our peers are on their journey compared to us and this motivates us to make changes, improve our learning or try out new things," says Marisa. However, the damage happens when we also use this assessment to determine how we fall short – for those struggling with low self-esteem, comparison is used in an unhealthy way to fuel feelings of inadequacy.

"We may wonder why we are unable to do the same as those who appear to have it all," says Marisa. "It's common to wear a 'mask' of success when trying to stay on track with everyone else, which can lead to even more pressure – feeding a cycle of anxiety and self-loathing." »

LIVE YOURSELF HAPPY

FREE YOURSELF FROM THE CYCLE

Here's how to prevent comparison and feelings of insecurity from sabotaging your wellbeing

1. STAY IN YOUR LANE
Focus on your own goals and work on achieving them in your own time. "Put together a plan, map it out, set realistic timelines, and stay consistent," says Marisa. "Avoid getting distracted by the 'noise' of what others are doing, as this can be demotivating and you'll be less likely to achieve your targets."

2. SPEAK YOUR FEELINGS
After spending the evening with a loved-up couple, would you question whether your own relationship is on the rocks? If you notice negative spiralling thoughts such as these, say them out loud to yourself, suggests Dawn. "What we accept from our internal voice often sounds ridiculous when spoken." This trick will help you to snap out of rumination.

3. GET CURIOUS
Look out for 'emotional landmines'. Having strong emotions when comparing yourself to others is your brain's way of sending you an important message, says Dawn. "When you have that twinge of comparison, bring it to the conscious and challenge it. Ask yourself, 'What am I feeling?' and 'Where does this stem from?' Almost all reactions of this type come down to fear and lack of self-esteem.'

4. PRACTISE AUTHENTICITY
Aim to be true to yourself both in person and online. "This is important, as comparison encourages a competitive 'keeping up with the Joneses' attitude," says Dawn. Be aware of your role in this cycle and try to live your life unapologetically as you are – it will then become easier to recognise when you are pitting yourself against others.

5. UNFOLLOW UNHELPFUL SOCIAL MEDIA
Is scrolling old school friends on Facebook your guilty pleasure? Do you often dig for info about your neighbours to see how they stack up? "Recognise this behaviour for what it is and shut down opportunities to spiral into comparison-led self-pity," says Dawn. "It's very easy to search for self-esteem-sabotaging evidence." Unfollow or mute unhelpful social media accounts, and question your motivation when being nosy about others.

6. BE YOUR OWN CHEERLEADER
Write down a list of your strengths and positive qualities. "This can seem an alien concept as we're hardwired to be humble and celebrating yourself may feel like 'bragging' – but it's not," says Marisa. "It boosts your self-esteem and reminds you why you are a wonderful human being and how you contribute to the world." At times when comparing yourself to others makes you doubt your worth, come back to this list.

7. BE REALISTIC
People often only share positive highlights, which is what you may be comparing yourself to. So, if you're feeling envious or disheartened by the fantastic lives of others, Marisa encourages you to remember that you're likely only seeing a snapshot – not the full picture. Everybody has a 'behind the scenes' version of their life, complete with good and bad days.

*Personality and Social Psychology Bulletin

WHEN GOSSIP IS *Good*

It can be surprisingly helpful for your mental health

WORDS NATALIA LUBOMIRSKI

Few of us can resist sharing a bit of chit-chat about other people – according to the experts, 60% of adult conversations are about someone who isn't there. But now we can enjoy this guilty pleasure, because science says that there are benefits to having a good blabber behind closed doors.

Social super glue
Gossiping is one of the easiest ways to connect with others, as confiding in someone provides the ultimate binding tool. "It's a great way to demonstrate common values and sense of humour, as well as share worries and seek support," says counsellor Chloe Ward. "And having a mutual dislike creates a stronger bond than sharing similar likes."

It can also help us build personal relationships. "Humans have an innate desire to know about other people's lives," explains Chloe. "People are motivated to engage in gossip in order to bond, to entertain themselves, to vent emotions and to maintain social order within a group." It builds a sense of belonging.

Stress relief
Feel like a weight has been lifted off your shoulders after a good session? "This is because the frustration that caused you to gossip in the first place has been released," explains Chloe. Having a stressful day? Gossiping with someone and venting your annoyances – even for just five minutes a day – can help to reduce stress levels. Gossiping causes our levels of oxytocin (the love hormone) to increase, while decreasing levels of the stress hormone, cortisol.

Self-improvement
It may seem counterintuitive, but gossiping can sometimes improve your feelings of empathy. "It may allow people to understand a difficult personal situation that another is facing," explains Chloe. And hearing positive stories about others provides motivation for self-improvement.

> "IT CAN HELP US BUILD PERSONAL RELATIONSHIPS"

HOW TO KEEP IT POSITIVE

To stop your gossip getting out of control, follow these tittle-tattle tips:

BE A SOUNDING BOARD
Provide a confidential outlet for your friend or colleague to vent. It will stop things festering and potentially allow them to come to terms with the problem.

ASK FOR FEEDBACK
When discussing a person or relationship, ask your fellow gossiper to listen with the goal of providing opinions, ideas and techniques to help you approach the situation in a different way.

STAY POSITIVE
If your chatter often spirals into backstabbing and bitchiness, make a point of saying nice things behind people's backs instead, and note how it makes you feel.

WHY DON'T WE PLAY MORE?

It's time to embrace our inner child and bring more playfulness into our lives! And in the process, give our health and relationships a boost

WORDS JOSEPHINE HALL

Most of us spent many hours playing as children, whether it was daydreaming on our own, acting out scenes with toys, or chasing each other during breaks at school. We shrieked with laughter, covered our eyes and counted to ten, created entire imaginary worlds... and we often didn't need much instruction, or persuasion that play was a worthwhile and necessary activity.

But as we grow up, we place less and less importance on play. It starts to seem silly, a waste of precious time, or maybe even a little embarrassing.

However, in recent years, there seems to have been a shift in thinking, with adult play becoming more popular. The video game industry, which has adults in their 20s, 30s and 40s as its primary consumers, has grown. Role-playing games have also increased in popularity, and game conventions worldwide have reported record attendance numbers. In 2007, Real Escape Game was developed in Japan by 35-year-old Takao Kato and since then 'escape rooms' – where teams of adults solve puzzles to escape a locked room within a time limit – have had increasing commercial success. In November 2019, there were estimated to be more than 50,000 escape rooms worldwide.

In a 2020 article for the British Psychological Society, researcher and board game designer Dave Neale wrote, "It has been claimed that we are in a golden age for board games. I would go further: we are in a golden age of play for adults."

What is 'adult play'?
Over the years, there have been many attempts to define what play is, but there are five characteristics that are widely agreed upon. Author and research professor Dr Peter Gray explained in 2013, "An activity

> 66 IT STARTS TO SEEM SILLY, A WASTE OF PRECIOUS TIME, OR MAYBE EVEN EMBARRASSING 99

HOW DOES PLAY PROMOTE LEARNING?

In 1964, Dr Marian Diamond, a pioneering scientist and educator who would go on to be considered one of the founders of modern neuroscience, and her colleagues, published an exciting paper about brain growth in rats. The scientists separated pairs of rat siblings shortly after birth, placing one in an exciting, toy-filled colony and the other in solitary confinement.

They discovered that the rats raised in a playful environment had thicker cerebral cortices than the others. Subsequent research confirmed it – the rats raised in stimulating environments had bigger brains, and were able to find their way through mazes more quickly. In other words, they were more intelligent. Ethical considerations prevent similar experiments on humans, but it seems likely that our brains respond to play in similar ways. Some circumstantial evidence suggests similar: Chinese and Japanese students are among the best achievers in the world, and they take regular breaks every 50 minutes.

can be characterised as play, or described as playful, to the degree that it contains the characteristics listed here: Play is activity that is self-chosen and self-directed; intrinsically motivated; guided by mental rules; imaginative; and conducted in an active, alert, but relatively non-stressed frame of mind."

Dr Stuart Brown is an author, psychiatrist, doctor and founder of the National Institute for Play in the United States. He is reluctant to define play, comparing the idea to over-analysing a joke and taking the joy out of it. Instead, in his 2010 book *Play: How It Shapes the Brain, Opens the Imagination, and Invigorates the Soul*, he asks the reader to »

WHY DON'T WE PLAY MORE?

consider what the world would be like *without* play: "It's not just an absence of games or sports. Life without play is life without books, without movies, art, music, jokes, dramatic stories. Imagine a world with no flirting, no day-dreaming, no comedy, no irony." He goes on to compare play to oxygen, writing "...it's all around us, yet goes mostly unnoticed or unappreciated until it is missing."

How do we play?
In his TED Talk, *Play is more than just fun*, Dr Brown outlines the five play archetypes that he has observed during his years of research:

Rough-and-Tumble Play
Such as tug-of-war, scavenger hunts or dodge ball. Through this form of play, we develop emotional regulation as well as cognitive, emotional and physical mastery.

Ritual Play
Activities or sports with set rules and structures. It's through these activities that people come together for a common purpose or goal.

Imaginative Play
Colouring, storytelling, crafting or even improvisation classes or stand-up comedy. Imaginative play is about living out fantasies and honouring our instinctual creative nature.

Body Play
Dr Brown describes body play as "a spontaneous desire to get ourselves out of gravity." It includes activities like hiking, yoga, snorkelling or even just dancing around your home.

Object Play
This describes anything involving manipulation of objects, building or designing, such as playing with Lego, building fortresses or snowball fights.

IDEAS TO TRY

TRY A NEW SPORT
Give a new, fun, non-competitive sport a try. Pick something you would have enjoyed as a child, which is difficult to take too seriously, such as hula-hooping, rollerblading, rock-climbing, paddle-boarding, skipping with a rope or jumping over makeshift hurdles. Yoga is a form of exercise that encourages play, especially acro-yoga – a combination of yoga and acrobatics!

EXPERIMENT WITH A THEME
A themed night/day/hour could be a solo activity or something you do with your partner, family or group of friends. Choose a theme, such as a country or a time in history, and get into character. Pick the food you eat, the music you play, the clothes you wear, the activity you do, all according to the chosen theme.

DANCE
Make a playlist of your favourite songs to dance to. If you're unsure, you could search in places like Spotify or YouTube to find dancing playlists, or ask a friend. Clear some space, dim the lights, close the curtains or wear headphones if it'll help you to switch off the outside world. Then just let loose and go for it! Dance as if your life depends on it and, most importantly, enjoy yourself!

GET ARTY
Encourage your inner child by engaging in creative play that involves self-expression. This could be drawing, painting or colouring in – the end result is not what's important, but the process itself. Collaging can be a therapeutic activity. Use whatever you have around the house, get cutting and sticking, and have some fun! Or get out and about and take some photographs – you could even make a short film, or learn a new instrument.

WALK BAREFOOT OUTSIDE
As kids, we didn't think twice about running around without shoes. Barefoot walking has lots of proven mental and physical health benefits, and it encourages both mindfulness and playfulness. When we are in a state of play, we are fully existing in the present, rather than worrying about the past or the future. Of course, sometimes it's not safe or sanitary to do so. But if it is, throw off your shoes and embrace any urges for 'oohhs' and 'aahhs' as your toes sink into the feel of different textures and surfaces.

The benefits of adult play

Playing is widely credited as a vital part of children's development, important for their general health and wellbeing. But we don't always realise how much these benefits continue into adulthood. Here are just some of the reasons play is good for us, at any age:

Reduces stress
The more stressful our lives become, the more crucial it is to make time for play. It can release endorphins – the body's natural chemicals – that relieve pain, boost wellbeing, promote happiness and relieve stress.

Stimulates creativity and general brain function
Play has been shown to improve memory, stimulate the growth of the cerebral cortex and even trigger the secretion of brain-derived neurotrophic factor (BDNF), a substance essential for the growth of brain cells. Playing also increases our imagination, which helps us to create new things, learn new skills, and problem solve. Just as young children learn best when playing, adults do too.

Improves social skills and connection to others
Playing with others tends to be fun. It can also increase our levels of empathy, trust, compassion and intimacy. It doesn't have to be a specific activity – adopting a playful state of mind could help us to cooperate, break the ice with strangers, or maintain existing relationships.

Increases productivity and reduces burnout at work
Google is well known for its inclusion of play in the workplace. Plenty of wall space to doodle on, and even staff play areas, help Google staff to be more productive. Regularly playing can help relieve the stress of deadlines and other work-related activities that cause tension.

Helps to keep us young
Play can boost energy levels and even improve our resistance to disease. As the playwright George Bernard Shaw once said, "We don't stop playing because we grow old; we grow old because we stop playing."

Why don't adults play?

The right to play for children is specifically protected by the UN Convention on the Rights of the Child, but there's not an equivalent for adults. Although the mainstream popularity of intentional adult play seems to be increasing, it can still be seen as a luxury that many people feel they don't have the time, money or even right to partake in.

Also, as we gain more responsibilities and life begins to feel more serious, we tend to become more self-conscious or afraid of embarrassing ourselves.

At the 2008 Serious Play conference, designer Tim Brown spoke about the powerful relationship between creative thinking and play. He began his talk by doing an exercise that Bob McKim, a creativity researcher, used to do with his students. He asked them to draw the person who sat next to them, in just 30 seconds. There was a lot of laughter as Brown's audience showed each other their drawings, as well as a lot of 'I'm sorry', which Brown said happens every time this experiment is done with adults.

With children, on the other hand, it's a different story: "If you try the same exercise with kids, they have no embarrassment at all," Brown explains. "But as they learn to become adults, they become much more sensitive to the opinions of others, and they lose that freedom... And in studies of kids playing, it's been shown time after time that kids who feel secure, who are in a kind of trusted environment – they're the ones that feel most free to play."

The same goes for adults. If somebody is experiencing difficult living circumstances, then taking time out to play could well feel impossible. Dr Stuart Brown spoke on the *On Being* podcast in 2014, and described how play "emerges innately and spontaneously if the individual... is safe and well fed."

Encouragingly, there are organisations such as Clowns Without Borders who bring their playful performances and activities to places around the world where day-to-day life is a tremendous struggle, such as refugee camps and crisis zones.

> **"THERE ARE STEPS WE CAN TAKE TO CREATE MORE PLAY TIME"**

How can we insert more playfulness into our lives?

For most of us, there are simple steps we can take to create more play time:

Give yourself permission
Remember that play is important for our health and wellbeing. Allow yourself to do it, in some way, every day.

It's all about perception
You might need to change how you think about play. Play could be something like talking to your dog while cooking as if you're presenting a cookery show, or making up a silly song while you shower each morning.

Learn about your own play history
In his book *Play*, Dr Brown suggests that readers "mine [their past] for play memories." Think about what you did for fun as a child, consider whether you did it alone or with others. How can you re-create something similar today?

Play with your loved ones
Insert playfulness into your interactions with your friends and family, and in romantic relationships, and see how it changes how you feel about each other and your time together. If you have kids in your life, follow their lead! As Dr Brown writes, "Play is the purest expression of love."

Let play refresh your life
We all deserve to forget about our work, responsibilities and troubles for some time each day. Play can help us to do that. Follow your instincts and your curiosities, and let play insert a fresh sense of energy and wonder into your life.

15 WAYS TO MAKE *LIFE* More Fun

Boredom got you down? Try these happiness hacks to boost your wellbeing

WORDS ALI HORSFALL

Whether you're feeling run down or life feels a little bit like Groundhog Day, you might be wondering how you can feel lighter and have more fun. But don't worry, there's no need to make any drastic changes. In fact, according to research published in the *Review of General Psychology*, at least 40% of our happiness is down to our day-to-day choices and activities. Here are 15 surefire ways to bring a smile to your face.

1 GO FOR A WALK FOLLOWED BY A SPRINT
A brisk ten-minute walk can increase self-esteem while reducing anxiety and stress, according to the Mental Health Foundation. Exercise decreases stress hormones while increasing mood-enhancing ones. And, if you add a 30-second sprint at the end, this doubles the endorphins and improves your mood for up to 90 minutes.

2 MOW THE LAWN
Chemicals released by a freshly mowed lawn enhance happiness and could even fight cognitive decline, according to researchers from the University of Queensland. Spending at least 15 minutes a day in the open air will also help you to keep vitamin D levels topped up, lowering your risk of depression.

3 DO SOMETHING SPONTANEOUS
Book a last-minute holiday or head for an unplanned night out. Changing our normal routine reminds us to prioritise happiness and that we have the freedom and power to do such things.

4 PUCKER UP
Apart from being good for your relationship, kissing your other half can make you feel happier. It releases the feel-good hormones dopamine and serotonin – the latter helps regulate our emotions.

5 TAKE A SNIFF
Vanilla is anything but bland when it comes to boosting your mood. Studies have revealed that breathing in its scent can elevate feelings of joy and relaxation. Choose candles and diffusers with essential oils and breathe in deeply.

15 WAYS TO MAKE LIFE MORE FUN

6 SAVOUR SOME CHOCOLATE
You may already reach for a bar of chocolate when you're feeling low, but there is some science behind it. The feel-good sensation of chocolate is due to a natural chemical found in cocoa called phenylethylamine, which researchers believe can create a feeling of mild euphoria, similar to the experience of being in love.

7 GO ON A DAY TRIP
According to psychologists at San Francisco State University, experiences make us happier than new objects, because the excitement of buying something new fades faster than memories. So skip the shopping and go on a short break instead.

8 GET APPY
Taking note of how you feel daily can give you a more positive frame of mind. The Daylio Journal app (free with in-app purchases, iOS and Android) lets you track your mood using emojis. You can also match your mood to daily activities and with the 'Statistics and Calendar' you can spot patterns in your moods and behaviour.

9 FAKE A SMILE
Flashing your gnashers could help lift your mood. Experts say that how we act physically can affect how we feel emotionally. The act of smiling can tilt your emotions towards being happy and is likely to prompt a smile in return.

10 ACHIEVE A GOAL
Whether it's submitting that work on time or simply getting that scrunched-up piece of paper into the bin, successes have a big impact on your mood. Set yourself a realistic and specific goal to help give you a boost.

11 EXPRESS YOURSELF
"Self-expression involves engaging in an activity that allows us to transfer the energy harboured in our thoughts and feelings into that practice, such as through words by writing journals, poems or stories," says neuroscientist Dr Lynda Shaw. "Self-expression can also be depicted in the clothes we wear or the music we choose to listen to."

12 CONNECT WITH OTHERS
After the COVID-19 pandemic, we're more aware about the importance of staying connected. "And not only can lack of socialising affect our mental health but scientists using brain imaging also found that when people experience social exclusion and social distress, some areas of the brain are similarly activated as if they were experiencing physical pain," says Dr Shaw.

13 LAUGH OUT LOUD
Many studies have proved that laughing can improve our mental health. "According to an article in the *Tohoku Journal of Experimental Medicine*, dopamine and serotonin levels can be altered by laughter," says mental health therapist Miyume McKinley. "They directly impact our mood and it's believed that these levels are correlated with depression."

14 TAKE A SELFIE
A study by researchers at the University of California asked students involved to take a smiling selfie every day for four weeks and found they enjoyed a surge in happiness, and became more confident on camera. Don't worry, you don't have to show them to anybody!

15 DANCE WITH ABANDON
Put on your favourite song and dance like nobody's watching. Research at Australia's University of New England found that participants who learnt to tango reported lower levels of anxiety, stress and depression.

LIVE YOURSELF HAPPY

THE Great ESCAPE

Escapism is often denounced as a waste of time, but are there hidden benefits that are being overlooked?

WORDS EMMA GREEN

Everywhere we turn, we are bombarded by negativity. Whether it be from a 24-hour news cycle, divisive politics, economic worries or the pressure to balance an increasing workload with a personal life, it comes as little surprise that depression and anxiety cases are growing at an alarming rate. No wonder then that people are more desperate than ever to escape in order to maintain their own sanity.

This is not a new phenomenon either. Humans have immersed themselves in some form of escapist activity for thousands of years, whether it be through storytelling, song or live theatre. The only difference now is that technology provides us with a vast selection of choices to enjoy. Entire industries, such as Hollywood, are dedicated to catering to the public's insatiable need for escapism.

Escapism can be defined as anything that detaches somebody from their immediate reality, usually through an activity that involves imagination or entertainment. The most obvious forms of this include watching TV, scrolling through social media, playing games, shopping, reading and listening to music. Even activities that are a vital part of our daily existence, such as eating food, having sex and exercising, can become outlets for escapism.

So why is it important? Because escapism is a deep-seated human need. Imagination is what sets humans apart from animals. Without it, humans would not be able to delve into their deeper consciousness, dream, re-live memories, create art or imagine new possibilities of being.

Escapism is also a powerful coping mechanism for dealing with negative emotions such as anxiety and sadness. It is a healthy outlet that temporarily removes us from an existence that can sometimes be too painful to bear. Without it, humanity would plunge into a persistent state of hopelessness and cynicism.

There is much comfort to be found in being able to escape into a world that provides a guarantee that things will turn out okay in the end and that the good guys will always prevail. Reality, however, is unpredictable and offers no such promise.

That is not to say that escapism cannot be used as a form of catharsis. Watching sports or listening to music can provide us with a platform to vent our emotions in a safe space without risking harm to ourselves or others. Video games, in particular, enable us to discharge tensions without any real-life consequences, and to flush out negative emotions through fantasies of invincibility and theatrical outrage.

It is important to know when to engage with an emotion and when to ignore it. Emotions are often fleeting, and it can be more helpful to distract ourselves from a negative emotion rather than to focus on it. Emotions are notoriously cyclical in their nature, and sometimes ruminating on them can strengthen the emotion and end up making us feel worse.

By allowing ourselves to detach for a while and shut off our emotions, we can give our minds a chance to reset and process matters more effectively. When we are overwhelmed, we can become blindsided by our problems and lose sight of the bigger picture. Indulging in some light-hearted escapism can remind us of the positive things in life. We are then better equipped to face reality from a fresher and more balanced perspective.

Escapism provides us with a boost of feel-good hormones such as serotonin and dopamine, an essential replenishment of the same neurochemicals that we lose when we are feeling stressed. This can help to dramatically improve mood and keep anxiety and depression at bay.

> **"ESCAPISM IS A POWERFUL COPING MECHANISM FOR DEALING WITH NEGATIVE EMOTIONS SUCH AS ANXIETY AND SADNESS"**

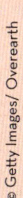

THE DOSE MAKES THE POISON

Escapism is a powerful coping method, but it can easily become a defence mechanism for protecting ourselves against feeling any discomfort at all. Too much escapism can lead to behavioural addictions, such as gambling or binge-eating.

It is important to differentiate between healthy escapism and avoidance. Positive escapism is a form of self-care, temporarily disengaging us from problems to re-energise, whereas avoidance can become a habitual way of ignoring our problems.

Avoidance is being so consumed by our chosen form of escapism that it becomes our primary purpose in life, rather than as a means of 'refuelling'. It can lead to problems at work, alienate us from our loved ones and cause us to stagnate in our personal growth.

We must recognise what it is we are trying to avoid through chronic escapism. It could be feelings of loneliness or boredom, or using it to compensate for a lack of interpersonal interaction.

According to Norwegian psychologist Frode Stenseng, two forms of escapism exist, depending on the motivation that lies behind each activity. Self-suppression (numbing activities such as abusing alcohol and drugs) comes from a desire to avoid unpleasant feelings, whereas engaging in self-expansion (activities such as meditation and creating art) are motivated by wanting to gain positive experiences and discover new aspects of the self.

It is vital that we strike the balance between using 'avoidant' coping strategies such as temporary distraction, and 'approach-oriented' techniques such as tackling challenges head on. Escapism is an important weapon in our wellbeing arsenal, but it is not the only one that we have to hand.

Escapism can also give us back a much-needed sense of control. By projecting ourselves through the personas we see on the big screen or in books, we can become the masters of our own domain and enjoy the sense of power, security and freedom that comes with it. Imagining ourselves as somebody who possesses something that we may lack, whether it be beauty, money or success, can be a powerful antidote against the disappointment of our own existence.

Furthermore, escapism can be a form of low-effort relaxation. Instead of viewing it as laziness or as a waste of time, we should look at it as 'refuelling'. According to Dr Michael Hurd, a psychotherapist, and writer for the website 'The Daily Dose of Reason', refuelling "refers to things of secondary importance that we do in order to mentally or psychologically recharge our spirits so that we can better handle the primary commitments of career, relationships or family."

Comparing our brains to computers can help to override the guilt associated with taking time out for ourselves. Just as a computer can overheat, too much seriousness and negativity can fry our nervous systems. Without escapism, we would burn out much more easily.

The great thing about escapism is that there is little effort involved and the benefits are often immediate. Recent studies have shown that escapism can increase levels of restorative sleep, awareness and social connections while significantly reducing stress. Paradoxically, it can also boost our levels of productivity. Escapism can provide a much-needed respite for our brain by encouraging easier thinking and a lower need for cognition. This means that when we do need to work hard, we can learn and focus better as our brains are not so exhausted.

Escapism essentially is about embracing 'mindlessness'. The concept of mindfulness and 'living in the present' has been all the rage in recent years, and while they are important for our mental health, so is the ability to switch off. Our society's obsession with achievement, success and busyness means that we can feel pressured to use our downtime constructively through goal-oriented pursuits such as learning a new hobby. But trying to be productive all the time is not good for us. Allowing ourselves to engage in a 'mindless' or relaxing activity for no other purpose than to unwind activates our parasympathetic nervous system, which slows down our breathing and heart rate. This can reduce anxiety and stress by creating a sense of calm within us, which can help to reduce blood pressure and strengthen our immune system.

So the next time guilt creeps in about spending all day binge-watching Netflix, remember that 'practising mindlessness' is a crucial part of our mental wellbeing toolbox.

LIVE YOURSELF HAPPY

THE THRILL OF Anticipation

Anticipation is an automatic emotion when thinking about future positive (or negative) events, but how can we harness its power to improve our wellbeing?

WORDS JULIE BASSETT

Have you ever felt that buzz of excitement when waiting eagerly for something to happen? That's anticipation. It can make you feel jittery or nervous, excited or euphoric. You might feel it in the build-up to a big event – Christmas, a birthday, a special party. You may experience it waiting for a concert or film to start, before you enter a bar for a first date, or as you step on a plane to jet off somewhere exotic. Our lives are full of small moments of anticipation, and you probably don't even pay much attention to your emotional response. But you should; anticipation can be one of the best feelings you experience.

First, what is anticipation? It's an emotion involved in awaiting an expected future event, and it can be both negative and positive. Negative anticipation is experienced as anxiety or dread, a feeling of unease, worry or fear about a future event. Positive anticipation is excitement, of 'looking forward' to something. Our body responds to anticipation both mentally and physically – that feeling of 'butterflies' in your stomach or a 'shiver' of excitement when thinking about a future event and its potential outcome.

Anticipatory thinking is another facet of anticipation. This is the act of anticipating how a future event might play out, which in turn helps us to prepare for it. We might anticipate various outcomes and scenarios, both negative and positive. You can harness this power to your benefit; by taking time to anticipate outcomes, it can help you feel more in control and calm about a future event. Our past experiences can help us to anticipate the future too, as we draw on what we know and have learned to anticipate the most likely outcomes to events. It's not hyperbole to say that anticipation is important to human survival – it enables us to anticipate danger and threat, and make preparations to avoid or deter these threats.

> **YOU ALSO NEED TO FIND WAYS TO ENGINEER ANTICIPATION**

Anticipation is an important function in our brains too. Research shows that anticipation in the brain produces dopamine, a neurotransmitter that's key to motivating behaviour and is released in situations where there is a possible 'reward'. We're more likely to anticipate positive future events than negative ones. When we have an underlying mental health condition, such as anxiety or depression, this may inhibit our ability to anticipate positive future events.

Studies show that positive anticipation can have great benefits on our mental health and wellbeing. One study showed that the bilateral medial prefrontal cortex was activated when anticipating positive future events, in comparison to neutral future events. The enhanced activity in the bilateral medial prefrontal cortex is associated with a higher level of wellbeing. Anticipation can be a very intense emotion, even more so than retrospect – the act of looking back at past events. According to one 2007 report, participants in the study showed greater 'evocativeness' of anticipation because they reported future events in more detail than the way they reported past emotional events.

How can you use this information to help you live a happier, more positive life? Well, by engaging the thrill of anticipation through ensuring you have future events to look forward to. Grab your diary and start making some dates. It doesn't always have to be big holidays and grand parties. Small, regular doses of anticipation could have an uplifting effect on your wellbeing. This is very much personal to you and what you look forward to. It could be a coffee date with a friend you haven't seen for a while, or a spa day at your favourite hotel.

Anticipation can also be trickled into your daily life too. Is there a particular book you are enjoying at the moment? Plan a time in your day to switch off, sit down and spend time reading. Then you will look forward to that slice of 'you time' all day, triggering those feel-good anticipation feelings. What do you enjoy doing and look forward to? Make sure you plan plenty of these small moments into your life, whether that's preparing to cook a favourite meal, settling down to watch the latest episode of a TV series you love, or arranging a date night with your partner.

You also need to find ways to engineer anticipation. In the modern world, instant gratification is much easier to come by. Everything is at our fingertips. But if you want to harness the powerful anticipatory response, you need to become accustomed to delaying gratification. None of us like waiting for something good to happen, but if you can wait a little longer than usual, you can flood your brain and body with far more anticipation. The reward is much sweeter if you have to wait a little longer to get it. At the same time, learning to wait a little can help us to refine our skills of patience and focus.

Why not try bringing a little more anticipation into your life and see if it can help you to feel more positive, happy and generally fulfilled?

REIGNITE YOUR ANTICIPATION

Have you lost that thrill of excitement in your life when waiting for future events? One problem with anticipation is that sometimes the thought of a future event is better than the event itself. This means that next time we're presented with a similar event, we don't anticipate it with as much joy, or we do the same things over and over again to the point where we know what to expect and therefore don't anticipate any different outcomes.

So how can you bring back that pleasurable feeling of anticipation? You need to mix things up! As adults, we're less inclined to try new things or break out of comfortable routines, but doing something new – or something we haven't done in a while – can reignite those feelings of anticipation.

It doesn't have to be big gestures; booking a meal at a restaurant you've never been to before can be enough to give you something to look forward to. Or you might be looking for a bigger hit by planning that dream holiday, trying a new hobby or joining a club. Pushing outside of your comfort zone reintroduces some anticipation and all the benefits it has for your wellbeing.

THE WANDERING MIND

THE WANDERING *Mind*

Discover how daydreaming can in fact be good for you

WORDS AGATA BLASZCZAK-BOXE

Daydreaming sometimes gets a bad reputation: students who don't pay attention in class end up having trouble completing coursework, and workers who spend meetings thinking about winning the lottery are probably not the most productive. But research has shown that not all daydreaming is bad.

"Daydreaming motivates people to work toward accomplishing their goals," says Dr Matthew Lorber, acting director of child and adolescent psychiatry at Lenox Hill Hospital in New York City. "For example, if a high school student daydreams about getting into a good college, such daydreaming may motivate him or her to actually study more during high school in order to get into a good college," he adds.

Here are a few other surprising facts about daydreaming.

> **"RESEARCH HAS SUGGESTED THAT PEOPLE ZONE OUT ON PURPOSE"**

1 WE DAYDREAM ON PURPOSE

Though people may think of daydreaming as something they do unintentionally, research has suggested that people sometimes zone out on purpose. Moreover, the circumstances in which such intentional mind-wandering occurs may be different from those in which people unintentionally daydream, according to findings published in March 2016 in the journal *Psychological Science*.

In the study, researchers asked people to complete an easy cognitive task, and found that the participants tended to let their minds wander on purpose and not pay much attention to what they were doing. But when the participants were asked to complete a task that was more challenging and required more focus, the people reported more unintentional mind-wandering, compared with intentional mind-wandering.

The researchers said they think that people intentionally let their minds wander during easy tasks because they know they can get away with not paying attention to what they are doing — it won't hurt their performance. But when they complete a difficult task, they know they need to focus to complete it well, and therefore are less likely to zone out on purpose. »

66 LIVE YOURSELF HAPPY

THE WANDERING MIND

LIVE YOURSELF HAPPY

67

2 BLINKING AND THINKING

Mind-wandering may go hand in hand with more frequent eye blinking, research suggests. In a study published in 2010 in the journal *Psychological Science*, researchers asked people to read a passage from a book and tracked their eye movements as they read. The researchers also tracked whether the people's minds wandered at random intervals throughout the experiment, or whether they remained focused. For this part of the study, the researchers asked the people from time to time whether they were paying attention or letting their minds wander from the task.

On completing the research, they found that people in the study tended to blink more during the moments when their minds wandered, compared with the moments in which they were more focused on the task.

3 DAYDREAMING CAN HELP WITH PROBLEM-SOLVING

If you are stuck on a problem, letting your mind wander for a bit may help you get unstuck. Research published in 2009 in the journal *Proceedings of the National Academy of Sciences* (*PNAS*) suggested that the brain areas that allow people to solve complex problems become more active during daydreaming. "Mind-wandering is typically associated with negative things like laziness or inattentiveness," lead study author Kalina Christoff, a psychologist at the University of British Columbia, said in a statement. "But this study shows our brains are very active when we daydream – much more active than when we focus on routine tasks."

The findings suggest that daydreaming may serve to distract our attention from immediate tasks to solve other, more important problems, the researchers said.

4 DAYDREAMING AMNESIA

For some people, letting their mind wander makes it tough to remember what they were doing right before their mind drifted. Research has suggested that such 'daydreaming amnesia' is exacerbated if your mind drifts further from your current moment. For example, it's more common when your mind drifts to memories of an overseas trip rather than a staycation, or to a memory of an event that occurred five years ago as opposed to two days ago.

In the study, researchers asked people to look at lists of words. They then asked some of the people to think about their own homes and where they had been that morning, whereas they asked other people to think about their parents' homes, which they had not visited in several weeks. The researchers then asked all the people in the study to recall as many words from the lists as possible.

The participants who were asked to think about their own homes were able to recall more words, on average, than those in the other group, according to the findings, published in 2010 in the journal *Psychological Science*.

5 YOU CAN BE ZAPPED INTO A DAYDREAM

Zapping a certain brain area may actually increase how often people daydream, according to a study published in 2015 in the journal *Proceedings of the National Academy of Sciences* (*PNAS*). In the study, researchers found that when they stimulated people's frontal lobes with a mild electrical current, the people reported experiencing more daydreams than usual. The frontal lobe is the part of the brain that regulates our self-control, planning and logical thinking.

"Our results go beyond what was achieved in earlier studies," study co-author Moshe Bar, a neuroscientist at the Multidisciplinary Brain Research Center at Bar-Ilan University in Israel, said in a statement. "They demonstrate that the frontal lobes play a causal role in the production of mind-wandering behaviour."

ON SALE NOW!

Take control of your mind for a happier, healthier life

Why do we feel certain emotions in specific situations? Why do we behave in particular ways? And what can we do to overcome the things that hold us back? Delve into the world of psychology and build a better relationship with your mind.

GET ALL 6 VOLUMES SO FAR!

Ordering is easy. Go online at:

WWW.MAGAZINESDIRECT.COM

Or get it from selected supermarkets & newsagents

FUTURE

WHAT IS LOVE?

70

LIVE YOURSELF HAPPY

WHAT IS Love?

From biochemical addiction to evolutionary perks, discover the science behind our most powerful emotion

WORDS AILSA HARVEY

The word 'love' is often thrown around and associated with almost anything we feel drawn to. Whether it is a person, an object or an abstract idea, you can love them all. But what does it really mean to love? Films often feature romantic love as part of the main plot. Its unpredictability, intensity and power make for an exciting storyline – just as it does in reality. While fiction often plays with an overly simplified, romanticised view of it, love is more than a fairy-tale dream. Love experienced in real life is a complex affair.

Where in the body do you feel love? It can feel like it is taking over your entire being, and most of your body does actually experience physical changes. Your heart is just one of the impacted organs, but it is also the one that we romanticise the most. As we come to terms with the uncontrollable feelings of initial attraction to another person, our hearts can get overstimulated. At the core of our being, it is one of the most obvious effects we notice. The heart has become the symbol of love, dating back as far as the Middle Ages.

The first feeling we may associate with being in love is usually euphoria, but from the moment you discover an attraction to someone to the latter stages of love, a range of sensations take over. From compassion and desire to obsession and anxiety, both positive and negative emotions can come into play.

What makes this feeling even more overwhelming is its uncontrollable factor. Love is felt subconsciously, to the extent that some people who are in love don't even realise they are. But love doesn't exist purely to add a touch of excitement to your life. Your body responds to further meaning »

WHAT IS LOVE?

relationships in order to keep the human race alive.

Although less important in our modern world of 7.8 billion people, when survival was more of a priority before the dawn of civilisation, the human body evolved to keep reproduction levels high. The ability to form this intense connection and attachment to another human being led to procreation and a parental team who were able to work happily together to protect their offspring and ensure that they thrive.

While the science behind love is intriguing to study, translating these reactions in the body into feelings is likely different for each person based on their body and unique experiences. Love has connotations of eternal happiness, but not everyone is built to manage these feelings. For two people to establish a trusting and growing relationship, being open to accepting love is essential. In the early stages, the body becomes vulnerable as physical and chemical changes induce a 'fight-or-flight' response. This is due to emotional strain being outside of comfortable levels. In some people who have experienced trauma, this fight-or-flight function becomes overdeveloped, as their bodies are used to danger. Each individual's brain needs to get used to rewarding the body with the chemicals of love. From there, connections with other humans can grow and be explored.

What happens to our bodies?
When we experience feelings of love, the following hormones and chemicals get to work in our bodies:

TESTOSTERONE
The male sex hormone
During lust, this hormone is found to be at high levels in males, while during the latter stages levels are reduced to normal. This chemical, which increases desire for physical connection, is essential for reproduction.

ADRENALINE
The heart-racer
Released in the body to prepare you for 'fight or flight', this natural stimulant is responsible for the rapid heart rate you may develop. Produced during times of excitement, it causes more blood to flood to the heart.

OXYTOCIN
The contentment creator
This chemical establishes a deeper connection. Skin-to-skin contact causes the neurotransmitter to be released and creates the close bond long-term partners share. This isn't exclusive to romantic love, and is also used to create a connection between parents and children.

NORADRENALINE
The attention-setter
Similar to adrenaline, noradrenaline gets the heart beating faster and induces feelings of excitement. However, it also increases your attention on one person and prioritises your short-term memory to keep you living in the moment through love.

VASOPRESSIN
The monogamy maker
Similar to oxytocin, vasopressin establishes part of the attachment phase. This particular chemical has been linked to loyalty between couples.

OESTROGEN
The female sex hormone
Produced by the ovaries as well as the adrenal glands and fat cells, oestrogen increases a woman's desire for physical contact during the lust stage. Abnormally low levels of this hormone can negatively impact general mood.

DOPAMINE
The rewarder
This neurotransmitter is used by your nervous system to send messages through the body. When in love, this chemical activates the reward circuit and creates a sense of pleasure from being in love.

SEROTONIN
The under-performer
During the attraction phase, production of this chemical has been shown to reduce. Creating a chemical

> "YOU WILL FIND YOURSELF ATTRACTED TO THOSE WHO DON'T SMELL LIKE YOU"

SNIFFING OUT THE PERFECT PARTNER

You might discover a lover based on initial visual attraction, their beaming personality that comes through during the first conversation you share or maybe even through a recommendation from a mutual friend. However, what you may not have known is that you are subconsciously analysing their genetic make-up. This might not be the first thing you grow to love about someone, but your sense of smell creates an attraction to people with a different immune system to your own. As an incredibly beneficial evolutionary tool, our bodies aim to partner up with someone with the potential to create offspring with the best chance of survival.

This is possible because a person's unique smell is created by the same sets of genes that make up their immune system, enabling us to detect differences in genes through scent. The saying 'opposites attract' couldn't be more applicable in this situation. While you may not notice the subtle scents of everyone around you, your brain does. More often than not, you will find yourself attracted to those who don't smell like you.

balance similar to someone with Obsessive Compulsive Disorder (OCD), this could be the reason some people show obsessive qualities during love.

ENDORPHINS
The painkillers
Released to create a soothing feeling, these are the body's natural painkillers. During physical contact with a loved one, endorphins increase and create a positive mood. Long-term relationships are thought to rely on this chemical.

PHENYLETHYLAMINE
The love drug
Released by the brain, this molecule stimulates the entire central nervous system. Naturally creating addictive properties similar to those found in the drug MDMA and coffee, this chemical creates the initial, intense feelings during lust.

The science of monogamy
When we think of monogamous creatures, we tend to think of scarlet macaws or swans, although despite swans forming monogamous bonds that last for many years (sometimes for life), they have been known to 'divorce'. Of the 5,000 species of mammal on the planet, between 3% and 5% are monogamous. This statistic means that species that remain faithful to only one mate or partner are in the minority. So why do so many of us fall in love for life?

We are not as monogamous as some animals, such as geese, who may not mate for the rest of their life if their partner were to die. However, with a significant proportion of our population looking to 'find the one', what happens in our bodies to keep us going back to the same person? Oxytocin, the hormone often referred to as 'the love hormone', is responsible for strengthening monogamous relationships. Creating a bond to the person you have connected romantically with, the hormone is used to reward the brain. The more intense response created makes any interaction with that one person feel better than interaction with anyone else.

Cases of a broken heart
Love can be the most uplifting feeling, flooding the body with feel-good chemicals and creating a strengthening bond of trust and infatuation. While these feelings can emotionally connect two people, it still doesn't change the fact that they are two independent bodies. Love can't be forced, and as many cases prove, it doesn't always last.

Heartbreak may be used to describe the emotional rollercoaster that is rejection, but broken heart syndrome is much more than simply feeling low; it's brought on by severe emotional trauma or a physical event of high intensity. While causes include some of the downfalls of love, such as divorce, infidelity, the death of a loved one and serious arguments, the syndrome isn't limited to love.

When the body is exposed to these situations, an influx of stress hormones take over. These are thought to cause the heart's main arteries to constrict in size, reducing the flow of blood in the heart. The effects of this usually include pain in the chest and difficulty breathing, but in a small number of cases this heartbreak can lead to death.

Q&A

DR MICHAEL MERZENICH
As a pioneering neuroscientist, Dr Merzenich has been granted close to 100 patents. Using five decades of research into brain plasticity, he explains the brain's key role during love.

Is love a real feeling, or a concept based on a series of strong feelings in the brain?
Love is the real convergence of powerful neurological effects that distort your emotional balance in a wonderful form. Our brains are designed to support that progression to love, of course. That critical progression to procreation and loyal partner support is key to the survival of »

HOW DOES LOVE AFFECT THE BODY?

Love takes over our entire body, from the chemicals in our head to the position of our toes

1. PUPIL DILATION
When you like what you see, your pupils get wider to allow more light in. This feature is part of the 'fight-or-flight' response to help evaluate potential threats. However, the love of your life often isn't a threat, and this response is usually linked to the production of oxytocin and dopamine, which are direct inducers of pupil dilation.

2. QUICKENING HEART
When you feel physically or emotionally stressed, hormones called catecholamines are sent into the bloodstream. At the beginning of a relationship, people often feel nervous excitement before seeing their partner. In this higher emotional state, the hormones released are responsible for increasing your heart rate and can cause your senses to be on high alert.

3. PAIN REDUCTION
Love is sometimes referred to as a drug, as it can quite literally act as a painkiller. When thinking of or spending time with a loved one, changes occur in areas of the brain that are impacted by morphine and cocaine. These effects usually happen during the early stages.

4. EXPERIENCING BUTTERFLIES
Conjuring the romantic imagery of delicate fluttery creatures, the saying 'I've got butterflies' refers to the connection between mind and stomach instigated by love. Cranial nerves help link the brain to other areas of your body, and being the longest of these, the vagus nerve connects to the gut. To create this feeling, the nerve triggers involuntary contractions in the stomach, caused by the brain's chemical response to nervousness. While it's not entirely known what the main purpose of this is as a survival mechanism, it could be the body's way of forcing out harmful toxins.

5. HORMONE PRODUCTION
Many of the hormones produced during love, while triggered by your brain, are produced by your adrenal glands. These are then released into the blood and pumped around your body in order to carry out their specific roles. During different stages of love, the brain is sending high volumes of signals to these glands, keeping them busy.

6. MENTAL HEALTH
Flooding the brain with an unfamiliar and complex combination of hormones and other chemicals, it comes as no surprise that love alters aspects of our mental health. Possessing a strong connection to someone else often enables people to manage stress, and can help reduce symptoms of anxiety and depression.

7. PHEROMONE FEELS
Unlike the majority of hormones your body releases, pheromones are released outside the body. While you are secreting these chemicals, produced in your sweat, saliva and urine, you are also picking them up from other people. Detected in the nasal cavity, pheromones can act as chemical messengers, making you attracted to someone nearby. It is this phenomenon that may explain some people's belief in love at first sight.

8. SWEATY PALMS
Through a combination of the hormones noradrenaline and adrenaline, your palms can turn into a clammy mess in nervous anticipation. Often you sweat when your body increases in temperature as evaporation works to cool you down. In these cases, your veins get larger. However, in the case of excitement or nervousness your veins constrict, as no cooling process is required. The built-up emotional stress that comes with seeing a love interest causes the body to prepare for a range of eventualities. Sweaty hands can increase friction, tactile sensitivity and skin toughness.

9. SYNCHRONISATION
Observations of two people in love have shown that we subconsciously mimic those we are attracted to. Whether we turn our feet to face them or mirror their body language, this demonstrates the empathy and unity being created between two people, a little like a pair of dancers. In some cases couples in love have even synchronised their breathing rates naturally by being in each other's presence.

10. LOWER BLOOD PRESSURE
High blood pressure can increase the chances of having a heart attack or stroke, so you could think of love as a health benefit. Although many see the early stages as particularly stressful at times, after falling in love people generally respond with less stress. Social bonds with a partner reduce stress, and with this comes a lower blood pressure.

our social species. Love is more than lust or procreation. It's also about stable bonding and enduring attachments.

Through the brain's reward process, is all happiness capable of developing into love?
'Love' is a sloppy word. I might 'love' football because I've seen my team have so many wonderful successes and celebrated them so cheerfully many times in my past. I have learned to associate football with rewarding. I may 'love' my garden or my pub or my job. This use of 'love' explains neurological attachment, but this is quite a different thing from the love of another person, where there are more physical and chemical factors in play.

That person has a rich array of ways to interact with me – by voice, touch and emotion – that reward and surprise me. It is this combination that can excite me. And every kindness I deliver to them that they respond to also excites me through the same neurological processes. When two individuals do this well, that mutual co-excitation is just about the most powerful way that your brain can be engaged.

Are some brains more susceptible to love than others?
Sure. The machinery in the brain is constantly developing. Its health and powers are a product of their historic use. We 'exercise' them as we live a hopefully stimulating and rewarding life – and some lives are a lot more positively stimulating than others. A person who has had a terribly non-rewarding life will take longer to find themselves smitten. In addition, a kind and generous person is exercising their brain in ways that help set them up for love.

What do you find the most fascinating about the brain's role in love?
It's all rather miraculous. And yet, it's still all blood-and-guts biology. As a scientist, I've been very interested in how our evolution of these processes can come at a price. The rewarding and stimulating processes can go awry, creating a major source of human suffering. Sometimes this can cause issues with mental illness, addiction, criminality and violence. How can a person both love and beat their partner?

We are a long way down the path to answering questions like that one. We are working to evolve strategies for helping individuals to drive their brain out of the kinds of ditches they can fall into – back to the thriving, loving human mainstream.

How much more is there to learn about love and the brain – do we have it all sussed?
Like many things in brain science, we have a pretty good understanding of it as a complex sequence of processes. We can see it happening in the brain through its major steps. At the same time, truly experiencing love is not the same as describing it through all of this organic biology, and it comes in diverse forms. I was very lucky to experience it as a young man – in my case with a mate for life – then with our progeny and their progeny and with my own parents. I have found love of different sorts, such as with a beloved friend and a dog or two.

THE 3 STAGES OF FALLING IN LOVE

LUST
During the lust phase, men and women release the hormones testosterone and oestrogen. Oestrogen is released by women and initiates a feeling of longing for physical closeness. Testosterone is produced by men, but females also produce it in smaller amounts. This hormone, like oestrogen, increases sex drive and establishes the first stage of falling in love. At the beginning, the purpose is to have a physical relationship, rather than an emotional connection, which is yet to be built upon.

ATTRACTION
The second stage continues some of the feelings felt through lust, but incorporates more of the emotional impacts. You will know if you have reached the second stage if you find your heart beating faster when around the person, you begin to feel nervous upon meeting them and you start to channel almost all of your attention on them. If you hear someone refer to being in the 'honeymoon phase' or saying that they have 'caught feelings', they are likely to be in this stage. This point in the process can instigate feelings of euphoria, but unfortunately it usually only lasts for a matter of months.

ATTACHMENT
As the relationship becomes more established, hormones responsible for human bonding come into play. Oxytocin is the main hormone responsible for the differentiation in this final stage of falling in love. Working to create a strong emotional attachment, this hormone is released along with dopamine – the hormone responsible for happiness. As you have continuous contact with one partner, the levels of dopamine released alongside the oxytocin provide a sense of reward and keep couples returning back to the same person. This stage also establishes a sense of security and a need to protect the other.

> "AT THE BEGINNING, THE PURPOSE IS TO HAVE A PHYSICAL RELATIONSHIP"

THE GOOD ARGUMENT GUIDE

It might not feel that way at the time, but a good row can have a positive effect – if you stick to a few basic rules

WORDS EVA GIZOWSKA

An argument that has gone too far can feel like hell. One of you makes what seems like a fairly innocuous comment: 'On the phone again?' or 'What do you mean, you forgot?' Then, before you know it, you're in a full-scale showdown. There may or may not be shouting, tears, eye rolling or passive aggressive, snippy comments. You can feel your anxiety levels and blood pressure rocket. Things are getting heated – or chillingly frosty – yet, you're no closer to reaching a truce.

"If you've got a good strong relationship with someone, whether it be a partner, sibling, friend or a work colleague, the occasional argument can be a good thing," says clinical psychologist Dr Michael Drayton. "In a healthy relationship, arguments enable people to learn from each other. Once you've both had a chance to calm down and reflect, an argument can give you a better insight into how someone thinks or feels.'"

"Not all arguments are constructive though," says Dr Drayton. "There are a few golden rules and if you break them, that's when things get toxic. It's fair play to criticise someone's behaviour or disagree with their opinion. But, it's not alright to attack someone on a personal level – 'No wonder you're such a loser'. Once you start going down that rabbit hole, things never end well."

"There's some interesting research by psychologist Dr John Gottman that shows there is a magic relationship ratio of 1:5," explains Dr Drayton. "In a healthy relationship, for every negative interaction, there are also at least five positive interactions, such as showing appreciation, interest, affection and empathy. This can also be applied to friendships. We all have good and bad sides. So, even if you have the odd argument, as long as the good bits outweigh the bad, that's the mark of a solid relationship."

"We all have our own different ideas, views and experiences," says consultant clinical psychologist Dr Claudia Herbert. "So, it's

THE GOOD ARGUMENT GUIDE

"IT'S HOW YOU EXPRESS YOUR OPINION THAT COUNTS"

practically unavoidable to have arguments at times. Having different opinions is what makes us grow. A good argument can help you to see things from a different perspective. But, it's how you express your opinion that counts. There needs to be respect. It's also very important to have personal boundaries."

"It's one thing to have an argument where you strongly disagree," adds Dr Herbert. "But, if someone is being forceful, aggressive or intimidating, you've got every right to walk away. We all have a 'window of tolerance'. This is a term used by psychologists to describe the zone of arousal in which you can feel your emotions and bodily sensations, but still feel centred. But, once someone pushes you beyond your window of tolerance, perhaps by being bullying, forceful and abusive, you may either go into hyperarousal – a highly stressed fight-or-flight response – or hypoarousal, where you just freeze and feel numb. If you find yourself going into either state, you start to get out of your comfort zone. You're no longer able to process or deal with the situation and your best tactic is to take time out."

How to have a healthy argument
Next time things get fiery, remember these rules...

What do you want to achieve?
"If someone upsets you, don't respond with a knee-jerk reaction," says Dr Drayton. "Consider exactly why you feel so angry or hard done by. For example, you might say 'you're always on the phone', but what you mean is you want them to pay you more attention. That opens up a new conversation, rather than just arguing about how your partner is always on the phone."

Take time out
"In one study, people were instructed to take a break from an argument. When they came back, in 85% of cases, they found a resolution," says Dr Drayton. "The time out gave them time to reflect and reconsider. Meanwhile, those who carried on arguing failed to resolve things in 85% of cases."

Ask why they feel a certain way
"Ask them to explain their opinion in more detail," says Dr Drayton. "This is a useful negotiation tactic – it takes the emotion out of the situation and allows them to feel they are being heard. Hopefully, in turn they'll reciprocate."

Don't try to change someone
"No one has the right to dictate how other people behave or think," says Professor Macaskill. "So, if you're having an argument, it's important to remember all you can do is negotiate. It's very easy to say hurtful things, but you can't un-say them. The main thing is to try and treat people the same way you would like them to treat you."

Take responsibility for your own emotions
"You might feel angry with someone – but, it's down to you to choose your emotional state," says Professor Ann Macaskill at Sheffield Hallam University. "Remember, you're only ever one thought away from feeling differently."

Really listen
"Try and put yourself in their shoes," says Dr Drayton. "Most people, when they're in the middle of an argument, stop listening. You've got two parties where no one is hearing what the other is saying. Sometimes when you show you understand where someone is coming from, this helps to create a shift."

Be aware of your own non-verbal signals
"If you're angry with someone, even if you seem calm on the surface, you'll still be giving off non-verbal signals that you're angry or resentful," explains Dr Herbert. The other person will pick up on these signals. "It helps to stay as calm as you can. If you can't, be honest and tell them that you feel upset and need some space to think. Sometimes people trigger emotions in us that are nothing to do with the actual situation. If that's the case, just explain that this argument has brought stuff up for you, but it's actually not to do with them."

Be quick to apologise
"If you feel you've upset someone during an argument, do apologise, and do it quickly," says Professor Macaskill. "Sometimes, all someone wants is an apology and by doing so, and meaning it, it makes it easier to move on."

Build BETTER relationships

You may not have the ability to change other people but you do have the power to improve your relationship with them

BUILD BETTER RELATIONSHIPS

WORDS SARA NIVEN

How do you get on with those around you – your partner, children, parents, siblings, even colleagues at work? Would you describe your relationships as good in the main or do things often feel strained with definite room for improvement?

Although when we talk about relationships in general, romantic ones first tend to spring to mind, but our attachments and interactions with other people in our life can be similarly significant.

"Relationships are key to our health and happiness and give meaning and purpose to our lives," confirms chartered clinical psychologist and author Dr Jessamy Hibberd. "We're highly social beings and early humans needed to live together and get on in a group to ensure survival. This means we have a deep need for social inclusion and research shows that a lack of social support is as bad for you as smoking. Social isolation is associated with heightened risk of disease and early death, whereas warm and supportive relationships have long-term benefits for health and longevity."

If a relationship isn't going well, we may find ourselves harbouring feelings of anger, resentment, guilt or general sadness, depending on the situation and how it impacts on us. For a relationship that has seriously broken down, be this due to a betrayal, major disagreement or other factors such as drug or alcohol addiction, professional help may be the best option to try to work through it, either by seeing a counsellor alone or ideally in the form of couples or family therapy. Unfortunately though, even with the best will in the world, sometimes it can be healthier to walk away (easier with some types of relationships than others, of course).

The good news is that when it comes to the daily niggles and gripes everyone has or unhelpful patterns of communication we may have fallen into with our nearest and dearest, a lot can be done to improve matters.

Here we look at five factors to bear in mind for building better relationships.

Lend an ear
Possibly one of the most powerful tools in the relationship improvements box, active listening is very different from sitting nodding, wondering when you will get your chance »

WHEN TO SEEK PROFESSIONAL HELP

However hard one person tries, sometimes it's not enough to get a relationship back on track, and it can be worth seeking professional help if you want to try to salvage it.

"Every relationship has ups and downs, and arguments in themselves aren't necessarily a bad or unhealthy thing if they lead to issues being resolved," says Dee Holmes of Relate. "When something seems to be continually looping around however, and arguments become less about practicalities and more of a personal attack with insults and resentment building, that is a red flag warning sign. Counselling with a qualified couple or family therapist can provide a safe space, free from distractions for people to start to get to the bottom of what the real issues are and how to work through them. It ensures a discussion doesn't escalate into just another row and the counsellor can reflect back what they are seeing going on to help additionally."

To find out more about Relate and the services offered, visit www.relate.org.uk.

BUILD BETTER RELATIONSHIPS

to speak or carry on with whatever you were doing. And it is the complete opposite of muttering 'Uh huh,' while browsing your phone as someone tries to tell you about their day.

"We have so many pressures, distractions and pulls on our attention that it can be difficult to be fully present even with those closest to us but ensuring someone feels heard and understood is really important,"
confirms Dr Hibberd, author of *The Imposter Cure*, (Octopus, £12.99).

Pointers for active listening include good eye contact (not staring intently, which can be intimidating), open body language (leaning towards the other person and avoiding crossed arms and legs), and an awareness of when to respond and when to stay quiet.

It's important not to interrupt or immediately override someone's story with one of your own – 'You think that was a bad day, that's nothing – wait 'til you hear mine!'.

Instead, when they finish speaking, try showing that you have been listening by summing up what they've been saying without judgement and with an invitation for them to continue. 'So, it sounds as though you felt disappointed today because you didn't get the feedback you were hoping and had worked hard for?'.

For something seemingly so simple, active listening can take practice (it is a learned skill when people train to become counsellors, for instance) but is definitely worth the effort in terms of the difference it can make in any kind of relationship.

A balancing act

Relationship expert, therapist and author Dr John Gottman extensively researched the secret of lasting, healthy relationships and noted that the couples with these clock up five positive interactions for every negative one. Dr Gottman even claimed to be able to predict the marriages heading for divorce based on this magic 5:1 ratio.

"The bottom line: even though some level of negativity is necessary for a stable relationship, positivity is what nourishes your love," his website states.

An interaction can be as simple as a loving touch or gesture such as reaching for our partner's hand or simply an experience of being listened to attentively, as described previously. A negative one can include something neutral like failing to make a »

> **" ACTIVE LISTENING CAN TAKE PRACTICE BUT IS WORTH THE EFFORT "**

CHILD'S PLAY

If you are a parent, building a healthy and trusting relationship with your child is probably one of the most important things you will ever do. You are effectively helping to shape another human being's self-esteem, and providing them with a good grounding for later life.
"When you communicate well with your child, it leads to a strong relationship, greater cooperation, and feelings of worth," confirms therapist Zinny Perryman, who has specialised in working with children and family interventions. "If the opposite is the case, it can lead to your child switching off, conflict and feelings of worthlessness. They are far less likely to open up about any difficulties or worries and it can be easy to lose touch with what is going on for them."
She advises:

Be as courteous to your child as you would a close friend. If you regularly interrupt them halfway through a story or break off to pay attention to something else, you are sending the message that what they have to say isn't important.

Unless other people are specifically meant to be included in the discussion, hold important conversations with your children in private. Embarrassing them or putting them on the spot in front of others will lead only to resentment and hostility.

Avoid towering over younger children. Physically get down to their level to talk face to face.

Use 'door opener' statements like 'That's really interesting' or 'Tell me more about that' to encourage your child to share ideas and feelings and show you are interested and respect what they have to say. Your tone needs to be genuine and your focus on them.

If you are very angry about something, unless it is an emergency that needs addressing immediately, wait until you feel calmer and more objective. Address the behaviour rather than labelling the child – they may have done something you view as stupid or bad but they are not a stupid, bad child. Your child needs to feel accepted even if their behaviour isn't.

comment on something our partner shows us as well as dismissive or critical statements such as shrugging our shoulders to indicate we don't care or rolling our eyes sarcastically.

Dr Gottman stresses that couples need to regularly demonstrate appreciation and respect for one another, something that sometimes gets lost over time. Although his balance theory has been developed to apply specifically to couples, there may be lessons that can be taken on board for other relationships given that everyone has a need for appreciation and we can all be guilty of taking others for granted.

Make the time
Without quality time together, it's easy to lose touch with what's going on in someone else's life, even when we're living under the same roof. We also have less shared, positive experiences to cushion the difficult times or negative experiences, becoming ships that pass in the night, or even ships set on a clear collision course whenever the sea gets stormy!

"Quality time doesn't have to involves hours, it could be as little as half an hour or even ten minutes in some cases," explains family and couples counsellor Dee Holmes, who is a senior practice consultant for Relate. "It is about managing that time and keeping it free from distractions. If your partner or child wants your company or attention and you have no choice but to take an urgent call or dash off for an appointment then be honest and let them know when you will be available for them later. But it is a good idea to build in pockets of regular time for family members – perhaps you decide that for half an hour after your child comes home from school you will spend that time uninterrupted with them or when your partner gets back from work you make a habit of having a cup of tea together."

While quality time can involve watching TV or a film together, Holmes stresses that an important aspect is the togetherness of an activity rather than simply people's proximity.

"I see children walking to school glued to their phones like zombies when previously they would have been chatting to friends walking alongside them," she observes. "Similarly, families can often be in the same room, all on different devices without any communication and it is something we hear complaints about in the counselling room. It can be a good idea to set healthy boundaries regarding the use of social media, such as no phones at the dinner table or during a certain time of day. These boundaries will be different for each family."

Dr Hibberd agrees on the significance of time and how it is spent. "Having experiences together is important in relationships, whether that's something major or something as simple as sharing a meal or a joke."

A FRIEND INDEED

A good friend is worth their weight in gold but when life is busy, how often do you manage a catch up? With some people boasting hundreds of 'friends' on Facebook, it can be all too easy for friendships to become more virtual than real. Perhaps you used to send cards but now it is much easier to post a quick 'Happy Birthday,' or you've been messaging a friend for months but neither of you have actually spoken on the phone for a year, let alone met up to see each other in person.

If this sounds familiar, it really can be worth making a little effort to bring a friendship back to (real) life. An unexpected phone call just to ask how they are, a card or ideally an arrangement to meet (that doesn't get postponed or cancelled so many times it never happens) can make all the difference, as will taking a genuine interest in what is going on in their life as opposed to only wanting to tell them about what is going on in yours.

You never know when you will need your friends so it is worth cultivating them and showing them how much they mean to you rather than leaving them feeling you only ever reach out in a crisis.

BUILD BETTER RELATIONSHIPS

> ❝ WE CAN'T ASSUME OTHERS, EVEN THOSE CLOSEST TO US, WILL BE mind READERS ❞

Explanations and understanding

Have you ever experienced a situation where someone stomps around, slamming doors with a pained, angry expression on their face, leaving you unsure if you have upset them, and feeling it is best to stay out of the way?

Later you discover they were stressed over something completely unrelated to you, or alternatively they thought they were sending out a clear message they were tired and needed help but you had no idea.

"When difficulties arise in a relationship, I often ask people if they have told those close to them how they feel and am often told they would expect that person to already know," explains Relate's Dee Holmes. "But we can't assume others, even those closest to us, will be mind readers. They may interpret a situation completely differently or not have a clue you see something as a problem as it hasn't been the case in a previous relationship. You can't underestimate the power of explaining."

She points out that it is also easy for miscommunication to arise when using text or WhatsApp, where there is no tone of voice or body language to help with communication. However, there may be times when writing things down can be useful in opening up lines of communication.

"For a situation in a family that continues to cause issues or arguments, you might suggest everyone writes down three things they feel would be helpful in resolving it and then sit and discuss them. Sometimes writing a letter to a partner, parent or friend could be a useful exercise if you find something very difficult to broach face to face or think they may not let you finish what you want to say."

Role play

If you've ever noticed that your interactions with different people vary and they seem to bring out different sides of you, welcome to the world of Transactional Analysis, or TA.

This is a theory developed in the 1950s that is used by some therapists to help explain why we think, feel and behave the way we do, particularly when it comes to our relationships with others. Very simply put, the theory involves three sub personalities known as ego states – Parent, Adult and Child – that we regularly switch between (with some further divisions within these, such as Nurturing Parent and Critical Parent).

It explains that we take on different roles depending on who we are dealing with and how we feel at that time, and it can be easy to fall into unhelpful patterns and roles. Realising we are doing this provides the opportunity to shift gears into a response that can improve interactions and relationships.

For example, if you are regularly annoyed with your partner about not doing their share of household chores, it can be easy to assume the role of Critical Parent and come out with an angry, judgemental statement.

Switching into our rational Adult ego state means we might say something like 'I feel I've been doing most of the chores this week and am really tired. I know you're working hard too but I'd appreciate help tonight'.

This invites the other person to (hopefully) respond as an adult as opposed to taking on the role of sulky child or becoming critical themselves and telling you all the things they feel you haven't done that week, with the risk of the conversation escalating into a row.

Our relationships, whether with relatives, partners, children, friends or colleagues, are wonderful things and enrich our lives. By being more aware of them, we should all get more out of our own relationships. ▪

LIVE YOURSELF HAPPY — 83

LIVE YOURSELF HAPPY

THE POWER OF Friendship

Strong personal connections in our lives can provide much more than simply companionship; friendship can shape who we are and enhance our overall wellbeing

WORDS JULIE BASSETT & LAURIE NEWMAN

"Friendship is the hardest thing in the world to explain. It's not something you learn in school. But if you haven't learned the meaning of friendship, you really haven't learned anything."

Those are the wise words of Muhammad Ali, who understood both the importance of friendship in our lives, as well as the difficulty of putting what 'friendship' means into words. It's a mutual affection shared between two people who care for and respect one another. Your closest friends are those you can rely on in times of need, who you can laugh with, whose company you enjoy and who you communicate with on a regular basis.

Our concept of friendship changes over time. As small children, it's not uncommon to make friends with strangers in the park after just minutes of sharing the slide. Best friends can change at school with dizzying regularity. In the social peak of our teenage years and early twenties, friendships can be extensive, part of a larger network of acquaintances and connections to have fun with. And then, as we get older, it shifts again. Our friendships are refined as we navigate through our working lives, marriages, children and reduced social time. If we're really lucky, there might even be friends that make it through all these stages of life, their stories interwoven tightly with our own.

How we make friends

All of these different friendships that we forge throughout our lives play a purpose, and ultimately help to shape the person we become. But they will all have certain elements in common. We usually form friendships based on two key factors: our environment and our individual preferences.

We tend to make friends by being in the same place, both literally and figuratively. Our first friends tend to be those people that we are at nursery or preschool with, or the children of our parents' friends. Throughout school, most of our friends are also our classmates, and later college friends, room mates and work colleagues. We might meet people through clubs and hobbies we take part in. We are drawn to people who share the same interests and who have similar life experiences to ourselves, which is why most of our friends are in the same environment as us and broadly the same age. We also gravitate towards friends who share our ideologies and beliefs.

In addition, we select some friends based on our own individual preferences. This can overlap with our environmental situations, especially if we're actively pursuing an interest and hoping to meet others in the area who share the same interest. But thanks to the internet, we can also 'meet' people who share these same interests online, and over time they can become true friends.

Types of friendship groups

Many studies have investigated the different models of friendship that we may experience. One such study, by Dartmouth sociology professor Janice McCabe, found that there were three distinct models of friendship types. While her research related to college students, it's thought to likely be representative of the wider population.

First there is the 'Tight-knitter', who is someone with a very dense group of friends, »

85

THE POWER OF FRIENDSHIP

who all know each other and are all closely connected. It's thought that this type of group is excellent for social support, but can be quite fragile, with disputes between members of the group affecting everyone and changing the dynamics.

Second is the 'Compartmentaliser', who has several clusters of different friendship groups. Most of us probably identify with this category, having groups of friends we've known since school, work friends and friends from our clubs or hobbies. This can be a useful setup, as we turn to the different clusters to meet different needs.

Last is the 'Sampler', who tends to have one-on-one friendships with a number of individuals, rather than groups of people. This can make a Sampler feel somewhat socially isolated and lacking a sense of belonging. That said, Samplers are often quite independent, not reliant on a group for their self-worth or personal success.

Whether you prefer group interactions and events, or one-to-one chats over coffee, when it comes to your personal style of friendships, the group that you most identify with can tell you a lot about yourself. The type of friendship style we're drawn to is linked to our own personality and behaviour, and identifying the types of friendships that we have can reveal a lot.

Someone who is quite introverted is less likely to have big groups of friends, preferring instead to have meaningful one-on-one connections. These can be less draining and more manageable for those who like the company of others in calmer environments and who feel lost in big groups – even those made up of friends. For someone who is more extroverted, having the chance to meet up with lots of friends at one time is exciting and pleasurable, energising and enjoyable. It might be that you like a bit of both – large social engagements and smaller meet ups with friends individually. Being true to ourselves means that we can get the most out of our friendships.

How many friends can we handle?

There may be limits to how many friends we can sustain. According to British anthropologist Robin Dunbar, we're hardwired to only be able to process a social network of a specific size. He set the number of people we can meaningfully have a connection with at 150. Through extensive studies of both contemporary and historical data, Dunbar found that 150 was consistently the maximum number a social group would reach before it either collapsed or split off into different factions.

> **"GOOD FRIENDSHIPS MIGHT EVEN HELP YOU TO LIVE LONGER"**

DIGITAL RELATIONSHIPS: A NEW MODEL OF FRIENDSHIP?

If Dunbar is right and we can only handle 150 personal connections at any one time, then where does social media fit in? We might have hundreds or even thousands of connections on these networks. It's thought that the brain can differentiate between the online chats we have with acquaintances and our face-to-face social interactions, but it still requires some of our cognitive power. This means that we could be expending some of our 'friendship energy' on these online connections, rather than nurturing our physical friendships.

Being online also takes up valuable time, leaving us with fewer opportunities to invest in our real-life relationships. This could, over time, erode the strength of our face-to-face friendships. While social media certainly has its place to help us feel connected, ensure that it isn't taking away from your real-world relationships, as these bonds have the greatest positive effects on your wellbeing.

THE POWER OF FRIENDSHIP

with more social support in their lives are more likely to make it to an older age. The results of some studies even suggest that breast cancer survival rates are higher in patients who have large social networks they can depend on for support.

Friends with benefits
There are practical benefits to having friends that can also impact your overall health and »

This might seem a lot, and you'd probably struggle to name 150 people off the top of your head, but this is the total number of personal connections that you could have in your life. This figure comprises an estimated five loved ones (such as immediate family or best friends), 15 close friends, a further 50 friends, and our more casual friendships make up the total of 150 meaningful contacts. Taking the theory further, you then might have some 500 acquaintances and 1,500 faces you can recognise. This is a range of values, and depending on personality type, you might have much lower numbers, or have more people in the early circles and far fewer as you expand outwards. This whole theory is related to the 'social brain hypothesis'. Dunbar argues that the reason primates have unusually large brain sizes in relation to body size is in order to manage these complex social systems – friendships are cognitively demanding.

The matter of who falls into which of these social circles often comes down to our frequency of communication with them. Those you make time for are likely to be your closest friends. The less you communicate with someone, the further outside your meaningful contacts they are likely to be.

"What determines these layers in real life, in the face-to-face world… is the frequency at which you see people," says Dunbar. "You're having to make a decision every day about how you invest what time you have available for social interaction, and that's limited."

Impact on health and wellbeing
Dunbar also stated in a later review that: "Friendship is the single most important factor influencing our health, wellbeing and happiness." It's no surprise then that those who are lonely are more prone to depression and other mental health conditions.

But how can something as simple as friendship have such a profound effect on us? In part, it's down to our brain chemistry.

Oxytocin is a hormone secreted by the brain's pituitary gland. This molecule is often referred to by the somewhat twee nicknames 'the cuddle hormone' or 'the love hormone'. Its effects are better known in women, as oxytocin is essential in the process of childbirth and nursing, as well as helping to form the mother-child bond. The same hormone is released in men too, which is one of the reasons that skin-to-skin contact is so encouraged when their child is born. Oxytocin is an important factor in building strong relationships, and enhances bonding and loyalty to our partners. It is also very important to our social bonding and friendships as it plays a role in the development of trust.

Another hormone that plays a role in our friendships is progesterone. It's also thought when you feel emotionally close to a friend, your progesterone levels are increased, which leads to improved wellbeing, and reduced stress and anxiety. It also helps to create strong bonds between friends, which is why you and your friends feel protective of one another. According to the NHS UK, stress can cause physical symptoms (such as headaches, muscle tension and stomach problems); mental symptoms (difficulty concentrating, feeling overwhelmed, worrying); and changes in behaviour (irritability, sleep problems, changes in appetite, avoiding people). Therefore, having strong friendships in your life can help us to manage these symptoms by improving our stress control. The simple act of having someone you trust to talk to when you are worried or overwhelmed can have a big effect on your wellbeing.

One study found that strong social bonds can also help you to stay sharper as you get older. Improved cognitive function in later life has been observed in those with high-quality social relationships and friendships. Added to that, good friendships might actually help you to live longer too. It's thought that those

MALE VS FEMALE FRIENDSHIP

In general, there are some differences between male and female friendships, though the overall benefits on our health and wellbeing are much the same. Male-to-male friendships are often formed more around a shared activity and tend to be less intimate. However, they are more robust, as male friends are more likely to retain friendships after a disagreement, for example. Male groups of friends can be more tribal, meeting up in larger groups rather than one on one. Female-to-female friendships however, tend to be based more on support, intimacy and connection. Women are more likely to want to spend one-on-one time with a friend, to have time to chat and communicate their thoughts and feelings. Women tend to require more communication with each other to maintain a friendship, and these relationships can be more fragile if there is a dispute. However, female connections are emotionally stronger and the bond is greater. This doesn't apply to all friendships, of course, since all our connections are unique, but these common traits have been observed in a number of studies.

LIVE YOURSELF HAPPY

wellbeing. For example, if you want to start a new exercise regime, you are far more likely to stick to it if you have a friend by your side. Or if we see a friend getting positive results from a new diet, we may feel more motivated to follow their example. We've already established that our brains are hard-wired to release hormones that promote trust and bonding in friendships, which means that we're more likely to mimic behaviours in those closest to us.

This can have a significant effect on our lifestyle. Whether the goal is to lose weight, get stronger, eat better or engage in more self-care activities, we're far more likely to succeed if we're doing it with our friends. In turn, these positive behaviours can help to keep our stress levels in check, lower blood pressure, maintain a healthy weight, sleep better and much more. All of which improves our health, wellbeing and mental state.

Of course, the flipside to this is that we are just as likely to mimic negative behaviours in our friends. If this is the case, it's worth considering whether such friendships are still healthy – or do the negative habits they bring into our lives inhibit our personal goals?

Another positive benefit of friendships is that they teach us a lot about ourselves. We often recognise certain traits in our friends that we find attractive, and from that we can start to build a picture of the kind of person that we are or that we want to be. We often select friends who represent the same values as us, which helps us to validate our thoughts, opinions and beliefs, giving us confidence and self-esteem. Our friends see us as who we truly are, as we're less likely to put up barriers or adopt a persona around those we feel most comfortable with, which is very liberating.

With such positive effects to having good friendships, it's important then to nurture those bonds with the people closest to us. It's said that losing a good friendship is akin to the grief of losing a loved one or a break-up with a romantic partner. Spend time with your friends, message them to check they are okay and show how much you value them, and you will continue to reap the rewards of the strong, positive friendships that you have forged over the years.

LETTING GO OF FRIENDS

As we embark on life's journey, we meet a lot of people along the way, but having too many friends can be exhausting

> **" TOO OFTEN WE HOLD ON TO FRIENDSHIPS THAT NO LONGER SERVE US "**

Over the course of your lifetime you will, without a doubt, meet a lot of people. As we navigate our way through life, some of these people we meet will end up becoming our friends. Friendships can form when we meet people at various stages of our lives, including when we go to school and university, when we start a new job, or when we participate in hobbies. But what really defines a true friend? What are the differences between acquaintances and life-long companions? And why should you hold on to some and not others?

The three types of friendships

According to Aristotle we have three types of friendships: friendships of utility, friendships of pleasure and friendships of virtue. Friendships of utility are relationships that have a mutual benefit to both parties and they are the more functional out of the three. For example, these could be a neighbour

GET TO KNOW YOURSELF

The one person who you need to get to know the most is yourself. Spending some quality time in your own company is one of the best ways that you can truly understand what makes you happy and what makes your soul sing. When we have too many friends, we frequently neglect our own problems as we become overwhelmed with everyone else's. We put our own problems and worries on the backburner – but this is wrong and this is when things can get a bit too much. Take a moment to organise and reflect on your own journey, and stop worrying about everyone else. Why not take a walk to your local park or spend an hour doing something you love solitary, such as baking or making music.

THE Power OF FRIENDSHIP

that feeds your dog or a customer at work. Friendships of pleasure form when someone shares the same interests as you. Finally, friendships of virtue are based on mutual respect and compassion, and usually form over a long period of time. These friendships are based on the idea that you share similar values and aspirations, and they can develop from as early as school years. But how are we meant to lead a balanced lifestyle with so many friendship circles? And is it possible to have too many friends?

Too often we hold on to friendships that no longer serve us, which is why it is important to take a step back every now and again to re-evaluate and ask yourself whether that friendship is of benefit to you. You have to ask yourself some key questions: Is this friendship making me happy? Is this person worthy of my precious time?

Time to let go
Maybe you can identify a relationship that is not making you happy and you frequently leave their company feeling sad. Perhaps you have a toxic friendship that leads to arguments and constant negativity. We hold on to certain friends for a number of reasons, but a common one is because of time. If we have invested significant time into a relationship, we stick with it. But whether you've been friends for one month or ten years, if that relationship isn't adding anything to your life, why waste any more time trying to fix it? Maybe you make an effort with someone and this isn't reciprocated – these one-sided friendships can leave you feeling exhausted. Like unnecessary objects in your home, it is possible and even recommended to cull your friends.

Less is more
Focusing on the people that matter the most is a step in the right direction. We need to free ourselves of the stress that is caused by trying to people-please, and instead focus on those people who make us happy. Choosing to have fewer, more valuable friends leaves you free from the unwanted pressure of trying to juggle your time between too many people. Pause for a moment and think about how you feel. Do you feel as though you are spreading yourself too thin? Do you want to invest more energy and time into people that matter to you? Then it's time to have a reshuffle within your friendship circle and direct your attention to the people who actually benefit your life.

The numbers game
When considering Dunbar's stance that we have 150 meaningful connections, 50 friends, 15 close friends and five loved ones, your true friends who are there for you through thick and thin are those you would include in this magic number five.

Take a moment and think about these five ultimate best friends, and ask yourself whether you are spending enough time with them. Dunbar believes that one of the main reasons we should declutter and refine our friendships is so that we can ensure our time is being shared in an effective and manageable way. Having a small, intimate group of friends means that you can hone in on why these friends make you happy and concentrate on building stronger bonds. Focus on these small, intimate groups of friends and be confident when you decide to walk away from the relationships that are no longer working. You will find you will become happier, more energised and better at managing your time.

LET IT FIZZLE OUT

Ending a friendship is never an easy task, but if you have identified a friendship that is no longer serving you, then it's one that needs to be accomplished. One way of cutting someone out of your life is by slowly reducing contact and the amount of time you are spending with that person. Start by not organising to meet up as frequently, and avoid texting back as often. It might not be easy and you will inevitably miss that person from time to time, but just keep reminding yourself of why you've decided to let go.

AVOID TOXIC PEOPLE

At some stage in our lives, we will inevitably meet someone toxic. Toxic people are draining and negative, and often the kinds of people who require too much energy and time. They are easy to identify because they can leave you feeling anxious and sad. These are the friends that we need to step away from. You can tell them your intentions by simply explaining to them face to face your reasons and walking away with your head held high. Be clear in the direction you are going in and walk away from people who don't make you happy.

LIVE YOURSELF HAPPY

THE Courage TO BE VULNERABLE

How can we embrace vulnerability to live more fulfilling lives?

WORDS JULIA WILLS

Humans have always needed to connect with one another. Indeed, for most of our history, fitting in with the group has been essential to survival by greatly improving our chances against food shortage, predators and enemies through co-operating. A safety in numbers. But even today in our modern, sophisticated and technologically savvy world, that instinct remains strong. We're still social animals.

From the moment we're born, we appeal to our parents for food, warmth, love and shelter. As babies we need our carers to respond to our every need to stay alive. We are vulnerable. We don't pretend – we let others know what we need by crying and demanding attention. We're real. Authentic to our feelings. But as we grow up, we become more aware of what others might think of us when we share our true needs and feelings, and we learn to respond to signals of how we're loved best – perhaps by showing good manners, being kind, liking certain things or achieving high grades at school; in short, by becoming the 'nice person' that people will like. In doing so, we often showcase the best side of ourselves to friends, family and colleagues, choosing to keep our less 'likeable' feelings to ourselves. In this way, we learn to forfeit being wholly true to ourselves in order to fit in. But is that the most fulfilling way to live?

Brené Brown, a research professor at the University of Houston, thinks not. For the last two decades she has studied vulnerability, shame, courage and empathy. She's written six *New York Times* bestsellers, hosted the podcasts *Unlocking Us* and *Dare to Lead* and shared some of her discoveries in Netflix's *The Call to Courage*. Refreshingly, she simply describes herself in three words: researcher, storyteller, Texan. In her TED Talk, 'The Power of Vulnerability', she candidly shares how she was drawn to social work, leaving a career in management at AT&T to search for a way to mend people's lives and fix the systems supporting them. Instead, she discovered that social work was about "leaning into the discomfort" and allowing others to find their own way. As a born 'fixer', it wasn't for her. Instead, armed with the knowledge from her academic studies that connection gives meaning to our lives, she chose to research that. However, what she discovered was that her research subjects insisted on talking about disconnection instead: broken hearts, being let down by others, isolation and shame.

Not good enough

Shame is something we all feel – save for those individuals who are unable to feel any human empathy – and it can eat away at us, telling us that we are simply not thin enough, rich enough, smart enough, fashionable enough, young enough, mature enough, pretty enough, athletic enough – anything at all enough – to be part of the group. Of course, our modern world is complicit in making us feel our perceived shortcomings.

> "WE LEARN TO FORFEIT BEING WHOLLY TRUE TO OURSELVES IN ORDER TO FIT IN"

⊢ THE COURAGE TO BE VULNERABLE ⊣

Every day, advertisements suggest what we might need to worry about before promising that their product is all we need to fix us, make us better and help us fit in more happily. Social media offers us the golden opportunity to play the comparison game 24/7, enabling us to measure our own lives against posts of others pictured in their best moments, encouraging us to fret about how we square up against our friends and celebrities. Not to mention the way we crave ever more likes on our posts as more proof of acceptance, but cringe when someone publicly disagrees with us or, worse, calls us wrong or stupid.

Brown says that shame nurtures an "excruciating vulnerability" within us. It's a psychological barrier that stands in the way of truly connecting with others. In continuing her research, she has become a world expert on vulnerability and, moreover, in revealing that by choosing to nurture and share it with others, we can live better. It's this groundbreaking work that she shares in her TED Talk 'The Power of Vulnerability' and her book, *Daring Greatly: How the Courage to be Vulnerable Transforms the Way We Live, Love, Parent and Lead.* »

THE COURAGE TO BE VULNERABLE

VULNERABILITY IS NOT…

WEAKNESS
Brown defines vulnerability as "uncertainty, risk, and emotional exposure." So, it's little wonder that sharing feelings like sadness might make us feel uncomfortable and somehow 'less than' others. Yet that same vulnerability enables us to feel happy things too, like love. After all, falling in love definitely comes with plenty of uncertainty, risk and emotional exposure. But just look at what it can bring in return.

OVERSHARING
Vulnerability isn't about attention seeking. It's not in the blaring headlines of another newspaper exclusive about a celebrity's broken heart. Brown explains that vulnerability is about sharing our true feelings with those people who deserve to know.

A SOLO EFFORT
We need the support of others to help nurture our vulnerability. But the good news is that sharing is contagious. Research done by Fuda & Badham (2011) revealed that showing our vulnerability to others inspires them to do the same.

Shame resilience
Some of us are more resilient to the shame we feel, a discovery that prompted Brown to investigate why. She called these shame-resilient people "wholehearted" and found that whilst they understood shame and its impact on us, what set them apart was their sense of feeling worthy of love and belonging despite this. Moreover, wholehearted people kept that sense of worthiness alive inside them no matter what life threw at them. She summed up their way of living as believing, 'Yes, I am imperfect and vulnerable and sometimes afraid, but that doesn't change the truth that I am also brave and worthy of love and belonging'. Essentially, 'I am enough'.

Of course, as she points out, this doesn't just magically happen. It's something we have to work at. Wholehearted people, she discovered, lived their lives with courage, compassion and connection each day. The courage to be who they really are, the compassion they show to themselves and others and the commitment to building genuine connections. Importantly, they "identify vulnerability as the catalyst." However, these findings weren't without personal cost to Brown. Comparing how she was living her own life to the way wholehearted people lived theirs unravelled her and she sought therapy.

How to develop resilience to shame
Whilst Brown believes that shame is simply too powerful to be overcome, developing a resilience to it is possible. Her research highlighted four things that can help us to do this:

Becoming mindful of shame and aware of what sets it off

—

Listening to what it's telling you. Are its messages about who you are and what you're doing really accurate?

—

Connecting with others to share your feelings

—

Talking about it

As Brown points out, these things feel like the opposite of what you want to do. You're more likely to want to hide or appease or get angry. Her answer, however, is to "trust the process." She shares how she deals with her own shame attacks: talking to someone she trusts, treating herself with the same compassion she'd treat someone she loved and "owning the story" - that is, accepting what's happened and choosing her way through it. By talking to people close to you, by asking them to listen, you may find them sharing similar experiences, therefore making that essential connection of showing empathy, and reminding you that you're not on your own. But it's in starting the conversation that takes the 'daring greatly' of her book title; the deep breath, the willingness to drop the façade and step out.

So, vulnerability is a good thing?
Most of us have come to regard vulnerability as a bad thing. A sign of weakness. Our Achilles' Heel. The Kryptonite that drains Superman's powers. The sunlight that turns Dracula to dust. The flaw that ultimately brings us down, whether warrior, superhero or immortal creature.

Yet Brown has discovered through both her research and her own personal life that engaging with our vulnerability brings us all the good things we really do want to have in our world – things like joy and love and contentment. Vulnerability, she concludes, is "the source of hope, empathy, accountability, and authenticity."

Daring to show up
Brown readily acknowledges that showing our vulnerability makes us uncomfortable. How could it not when it grows from emotions like sadness or disappointment or perhaps having done something wrong? All the things we'd prefer to keep tucked away to remain looking great on the outside.

Yet listening to her talk about vulnerability is empowering; the idea of "daring to show up and let ourselves be seen." She makes the point that, essentially, unless we engage with our vulnerability and the uncertainty, risk and emotional exposure that it's comprised of, then we cannot truly engage with others. And we need to start now. We simply don't have time to wait until things are absolutely right for us to take up the challenges in our lives, start a relationship with someone, change jobs or have that difficult conversation. In waiting, she says, "We ultimately sacrifice relationships and opportunities that may not be recoverable." For her, stepping into those situations, without guarantees, without knowing what will happen and risking the possible hurt, is a measure of courage: courage through vulnerability. So, how can we do it?

Becoming vulnerable
The answer, Brown says, is to lose the "vulnerability armoury," and to drop our weaponry. That's easier said than done, so it's heartening to know that she struggles too. Yet, by persevering she has found strategies that work, including:

BELIEVE 'I AM ENOUGH'
Recognising that we've had enough of comparing, ranking and endlessly trying to do better than others is a great first step.

> **ENGAGING WITH VULNERABILITY BRINGS US ALL THE GOOD THINGS WE REALLY DO WANT**

We can then allow ourselves to be seen and heard and know that we are enough just as we are.

DROP THE PERFECT
Perfect doesn't exist. So, aiming for it, as a perfectionist, sets us up to failure and disappointment and – yes, you've guessed it – more shame.

NURTURE SELF-COMPASSION
This is about accepting that we're human, that we have flaws and choosing to show ourselves the same understanding and support that we'd give a good friend. Sure, we mess up, but we are still worthy of love and connection.

LET YOURSELF FEEL YOUR EMOTIONS
Don't try to numb the bad stuff in order to feel better. Whether it's food, gambling, alcohol, shopping or medication drugs that take the edge off feeling down, disappointed or fearful, the problem is that numbing doesn't differentiate. We can't numb the emotions we don't want and still hang on to the ones we do, like joy and happiness and feeling grateful for all the good things that are in our lives.

EMBRACE JOY
Living with a sense of not being good enough can make us wonder if we actually deserve joy when it »

SHAME ON YOU

Although nearly everybody feels shame, Brown discovered some clear differences in what sparks the feeling in men and women. For women, it's about how they look, with feelings around motherhood coming close behind (something that affects non-mothers too). Worse, however well women are accomplishing the things in their life, there's still the unspoken need to be natural and modest about it all. Don't show off. Stay sweet. For men, it's about being seen as strong – everywhere. The necessity to not show weakness, to 'man up' starts early in life and goes on to permeate adulthood at home, at work, in sport and romance. In fact, one particular shame trigger for men was sexual rejection.

> **IF WE ARE PREPARED TO DROP OUR MASKS AND SHARE THE REAL US, OUR LIVES CAN BE MUCH RICHER**

turns up. Brown calls it "foreboding joy" – not being able to delight in a moment without wondering what the catch might be. The trick is to feel gratitude in that moment. Joy doesn't have to last forever. In fact, it won't. But by spotting those moments, those little things and allowing ourselves to really experience them, we enrich our lives.

Vulnerability and authenticity
Becoming vulnerable is about jettisoning who we think we should be for who we really are. Another area of study that resonates with this is the authenticity research done by Professor Stephen Joseph of Nottingham University in the UK. He is a leading voice in positive psychology and his book *Authentic: How to Be Yourself and Why It Matters* explains how we can flourish in choosing to live true to ourselves.

In his book, Professor Joseph shares his 'authenticity formula'. It comprises three things:

- Knowing yourself
- Owning yourself
- Being yourself

As with putting Brown's findings into practice, none of these things is easy to do. However, Joseph's book shares lots of practical exercises across all three areas to help us become authentic.

The first step, that of getting to know ourselves, is about understanding the things we do to deceive ourselves. This includes behaviours like defence mechanisms, for example, denial ('Of course I'm not drinking too much') or rationalising our reactions ('I didn't really want that promotion anyway'). Other behaviours that can stand in the way of seeing ourselves clearly include acting out (throwing our toys out of the pram) and displacement (shouting at the dog when you're angry with your partner).

Although defence mechanisms can be useful at times, perhaps getting us through tough times, they can stop us from really seeing how things are. It's not always easy to do this by ourselves and sometimes we might need help in finding our way. But, by noticing how our self-fooling behaviours can get in our own way and by listening to our inner wisdom instead, we can take that second step. We can choose to take genuine responsibility for the way we act.

Finally, it's about putting it all into practice, moment by moment. We begin to use what we've found out in the first two steps to re-build a more genuine self-image and live differently – say, putting in the boundaries we need, becoming more assertive with others and accepting ourselves for who we actually are. In this way, as with Brown's vulnerability, we can drop the constant ranking and comparing with others. Whilst Brown talks of "shame resilience," Joseph goes a step further in talking about "shame resistance," but both becoming vulnerable and living authentically share that same willingness to take a stand against shame doing its thing and holding us back from living better. Brown's wholehearted people believe that they are enough even though they know they mess up; Joseph's authentic people "recognise (instead) that different people have different strengths, talents and abilities and are all equal as human beings."

Vulnerability in the wider world
It's true that the world of late hasn't been any easier to live in. Wars, the pandemic, political wrangling, recessions – they all undermine our sense of feeling secure in our lives. And as Brown points out in her book, "rather than coming together to heal (which requires vulnerability), we're angry and scared and at one another's throats." She discovered this dynamic in play at work, in schools, at home, in politics and in the community at large, with the three factors of shame, comparison and disengagement at their heart. It's there in the workplace when we don't share the good idea we have for fear of it being dismissed. It's there in the classroom where the student doesn't feel able to challenge the teacher because they want to keep getting good grades. And it's in the home where parents want to do their best for their children but are still battling with their own sense of worth and inadvertently send messages to their kids about what makes them more or less loveable. If we look, we'll see shame, comparison and disengagement at work amongst our family, friends and colleagues, in our media reporting and communities, from the people we meet each day to those in the highest reaches of power.

However, it doesn't have to be this way. Shame in organisations can be tackled head-on if we are honest enough to seek it out and expose it and talk to one another. Brown sees feedback as essential and that it 'fosters growth and engagement'. Again, most of us might cringe about opening up in such a way, particularly in a professional setting, and Brown admits that people need training in how to give and receive it. Feeling discomfort is natural. But, instead of shying away from it, we can learn to normalise it as a part of the process. And that way, change is possible. The big challenge for

GLOSSARY OF TERMS

GUILT
Guilt is about doing something bad. For example, someone who steals something can learn that they did something wrong and can change their behaviour in future.

SHAME
Shame is about being something bad. Here, someone who steals something comes to believe that they are a thief and so has far less incentive to behave differently next time. For Brown, "Shame corrodes the very part of us that believes we can change and do better."

VULNERABLE
According to the Merriam-Webster dictionary the word 'vulnerable' comes from the Latin vulnus ('wound') and means being able to be physically wounded or having the power to wound others. More recently, its meaning has widened to include defencelessness against all forms of attack – physical, emotional and psychological.

AUTHENTIC
Authentic means genuine. In terms of human psychology, being authentic is about choosing to be honest with ourselves and living according to who we really are.

HUMILIATION
Humiliation is being made to feel 'less than' by others. It can make us uncomfortable, can hurt us and is often embarrassing. However, psychologist Donald Klein believes that humiliation is less damaging than shame and maintains that we can choose not to internalise it and that instead, by seeing the problem as lying with the humiliator, we can remain robust.

---

leaders of all communities as Brown says, is "to teach the people around us how to accept discomfort as a part of growth."

Again in the wider world, Professor Joseph points out that whilst there is no one style of leadership to fit all, what works well against a toxic workplace is an authentic leader who can see different sides of a problem, several perspectives and understand information in a balanced way. They can then express themselves without seeming manipulative. It's something we can all be a part of. We can all learn to actively listen to "people inquiring about what is happening in their lives and speaking truthfully about our own experiences while staying in the present moment," which accords with Brown's hope for the shame-resilient feedback that can bring about change for the better.

At home, being aware of shame can help us not to use it in moulding our children's behaviour. However, they're still going to encounter it when they walk out the front door: Not being picked for the team or invited to the party, or being belittled or teased. However, Brown maintains that as long as children know they can talk to their carers about what happened, then shame resilience can be nurtured and children can develop a sense of their own worth. A feeling of belonging to the family is central here – that in the family they can be who they are and they are loved for it. Of course, there will be behaviours that need changing, but the children know that they are wholly accepted. They are loved and belong unconditionally.

For Joseph, unconditional love is the balancing act between supporting children in developing their own agency and letting them know that they are valued just the way they are. Of course, children will still pick up ideas about what make them more attractive to others but parents can help children build a sense of true worth in the way that they praise them. For example, Joseph explains, telling a child that they are pretty or smart – qualities that the child has no control over – is less helpful than praising them for what they do have control over, for example, their effort or commitment. "Authentic parents," he says, "offer their children the freedom to be themselves and to remain loved for being themselves." Of course, parenting authentically depends on how authentic one is as a person and, just as in Brown's work, actions speak louder than words. As she shares, you can't tell your child that stealing is wrong and then joke with them about how the cashier forgot to ring one of your cans of beans through.

The courage to be vulnerable
The research shows us that if we are prepared to drop our masks and share the real us, our lives can be much richer. So can those of our children, our communities and workplaces. Our world can change for the better. Of course, neither becoming vulnerable nor taking the steps needed to live authentically are easy. Both take courage. We must dare to show up. And that's scary. But not, as Brown concludes in her talk ('The Call to Courage') as scary as "getting to the end of our lives and having to ask ourselves, 'What if I would've shown up?'" Perhaps it's time for us to find out.

THE MAGIC OF Hugging

Long periods of time without physical interaction can play havoc with our mental health – and there's a big reason why

WORDS FAYE M SMITH

The COVID-19 pandemic changed many things about daily life, especially in relation to social contact. In fact, more than a third* of British people said they would never take hugging for granted again. And there's good reason why staying a metre or two away from our loved ones hit hard and felt more than just inconvenient. "The reality is that hugging – an action humans have done instinctively forever – has a very real impact that reaches far beyond closeness," says psychotherapist and couples therapist Audrey Stephenson. "Through touch we soothe emotionally, regulate neurologically, rest cardiovascularly and connect soulfully. That's a whole lot of loss." Here's why a simple hug can be an instant healer...

Watch out for any warning signs
Oxytocin is also known to boost your mood, while reducing stress and depression. Signs you've been lacking an essential oxytocin release can be subtle, such as a change to your usual eating or drinking habits. "You may also experience sleep disturbances, lack of concentration and irritability," says Dr Meg Arroll, a chartered psychologist with Healthspan. "So, if restrictions mean you cannot hug loved ones, make sure to at least talk about how you're feeling with close friends and family."

The impact on mental health
80%** of adults in the UK said social distancing, or 'physical distancing', as the World Health Organization refers to it, negatively impacted their mental health. Yet hugging, if we're allowed to, could be a quick, cost-free solution. "Hugging has many benefits to our wellbeing," says Dr Rachel Chin, a clinical psychologist from the Pennine Care NHS Foundation Trust. "It triggers the release of the hormone and neurotransmitter oxytocin into our body, higher levels of which are associated with increased feelings of relaxation and security."

Why timing is everything
Most of us have felt it – that awkward moment when a hug lasts a fraction longer than we wanted, resulting in a negative feeling. "Our nervous systems respond to a hug, either with complete bodily relaxation (if we have a trusting relationship with the hugger), or we can feel rigid and trapped (if we don't)," says Audrey. Yet sadly, while there's no research to indicate the optimum hug duration, the length can affect the depth of the benefits received. "A quick social hug may act as a connector and bridge to feeling 'we're connected' and 'I exist'," says Audrey. "Yet as you relax into a long hug, you may even align breath or heartbeat with the other person, which can bring inner peace."

It all stems back to childhood
There's another reason why a cuddle makes you feel safe and secure. "Being hugged can tap into muscle memory from being comforted as a child," says Audrey. This is why not being given physical affection in early years can often impact adult relationships. "Human contact is vital over a lifetime," says Dr Arroll. "Without this bonding, we can grow to be insecure in adult relationships, or simply avoid them altogether. But the human mind is open to

> " HUGGING HAS AN IMPACT THAT REACHES FAR BEYOND CLOSENESS "

THE MAGIC OF HUGGING

EMBRACING THE FUTURE

With fears of other pandemics surging into society, the future of being able to hold loved ones close or giving a quick hug to welcome strangers is uncertain. "Other countries and cultures have different greetings, so it's not the only way to welcome others and show affection," says Dr Arroll. "As humans, we are very adaptable. What feels awkward now, such as an elbow-to-elbow bump, could, in time, become part of our physical narrative. However, research shows that although something like a virtual hug may be a nice gesture, it's unlikely to have the same psychological impact."

be the best dog breeds to improve anxiety levels in their owners***. "Stroking and cuddling a pet triggers a flood of oxytocin, so physical touch with pets can help," says Dr Arroll. The study also found that petting a dog for 15 minutes could lower blood pressure by 10%, and help with Alzheimer's and heart disease. Prefer cats? Sphynx and Ragdoll came out as two of the top depression-beating breeds, possibly due to the affection they demand.

change – so if you didn't grow up with a secure attachment, you can still develop one later in life through self-awareness or therapy."

Fight off a cold
Ironically, while limiting human contact stops germs from spreading, hugging can actually help you fight off illness. "There's evidence that hugging can build your immune system," says Dr Arroll. "One study of over 400 healthy adults found that hugging boosted protection against contracting a cold. In those who did develop a cold, greater frequency of hugs led to less severe symptoms." Although this shouldn't be a reason to ignore any government guidelines.

Get that 'feel good' factor back
There are some alternatives to hugging. "Smiling, making eye contact and gesturing, in addition to warm verbal expressions, can have similar benefits," says Dr Chin. "Try cuddling a pillow – spraying a calming scent onto the fabric may also help you to feel soothed."

Pets can make a difference
Own a Labrador, Vizsla or Poodle? They were found to

© Getty Images / Johanna Svennberg
*Higgidy Simple Pleasures Study May 2020. **Superdrug and My Online Therapy survey. ***Tombola

LIVE YOURSELF HAPPY

BOOST HAPPINESS WITH *Diet & Exercise*

Finding foods that fuel your brain and body, and moving in a way that feels good, can contribute a great deal to your mental wellbeing

WORDS JULIE BASSETT

Lifestyle plays a huge role in the way that we feel – not just physically, but mentally too. What we eat and how much we move can impact positively or negatively on our mental wellbeing, which is why it's so important to be mindful around diet and exercise. However, there is no one lifestyle template that suits everyone and has the same impact; there is an element of trial and error to learn what makes you feel happy.

Food and mood

There are two key ways in which our diet can make us feel happier: by eating nourishing foods that are packed with mood-boosting nutrients that directly impact on our brain chemistry; and by indulging in foods that we enjoy with people we feel connected to.

Aiming to maintain a healthy, balanced diet has a huge number of well-researched and evidenced benefits, which includes a boost to our mental wellbeing. It doesn't need to be complicated either – there is no need for restrictive diets or expensive regimes.

It's best to eat regularly throughout the day, which keeps your blood sugar levels on an even keel. If your blood sugar drops too much between meals, this can have a negative impact on your mood. You're likely to feel irritable and weak, 'hangry' even. Try to include plenty of fruits and vegetables – as many varieties as possible throughout a week – wholegrains and protein, which are all packed with vitamins, minerals and amino acids that help to nourish your body, fuel your brain and regulate your mood. It's also very important to have a good amount

> "IT DOESN'T NEED TO BE COMPLICATED – THERE IS NO NEED FOR RESTRICTIVE DIETS OR EXPENSIVE REGIMES"

GUT HEALTH AND HAPPINESS

We're learning more all the time about the gut microbiome and its connection with other functions in our body, including our brain and mental health. One review* explored the link between gut health and mental health, which suggested that the use of gut-boosting probiotics in those with anxiety or depression (as an addition to conventional treatment, not independently of) may be of benefit. While further research is needed, what we do know is that looking after the gut has a whole host of benefits, from better heart health and digestive function, to a stronger immune system and increased energy – which in turn will help with mental wellbeing. So, it's worth including plenty of gut-friendly foods in your diet, such as live yogurts and fermented foods like kimchi or sauerkraut.

of healthy fats, as this is essential to your brain function, so make sure that you include things like oily fish, avocados, olive oil, eggs and olives regularly. It's often cited that the Mediterranean way of eating is optimal, and actually this is fairly achievable for many of us. Meals can be simple, colourful and based around veg and good fats, plus it's easy to adapt for all dietary preferences. A colourful plate of food looks appetising and makes us feel happier too, and if there are lots of different colours in a meal, then there are lots of different nutrients too.

Ideally, we want to limit ultra-processed foods that don't nourish our minds and bodies, and focus on those wholefoods that have inherent benefits. For example, tyrosine and tryptophan play an important role in the production of dopamine, which makes us feel good, and serotonin, which regulates our moods. You can find these in foods like chicken, turkey, milk, bananas, cheese, pumpkin seeds and eggs. Other key nutrients include folate, which helps with brain function and is found in Brussel sprouts, broccoli and leafy green vegetables; vitamin C, which can improve or regulate mood and energy levels, found in citrus fruits and bell peppers; and B-12, which is linked to the regulation of our mental state, found in meat, sardines, tuna, dairy products and fortified products. »

BOOST HAPPINESS WITH DIET AND EXERCISE

DON'T OVERDO IT

Once you start to feel the effects of an improved diet or new exercise regime, it can be easy to take it too far. It's important not to become too restrictive in your diet, or exercise too hard too often – this can start to have a negative effect on your mental health, which is the opposite of what we're trying to achieve. There is a balance to find where lifestyle positively impacts on wellbeing. This means enjoying your food, eating those things that are less healthy in moderation, and looking at your nutrition over a whole week and not just a single day. It also means ensuring that you're taking enough rest between harder exercises sessions, and taking time for gentler activities like walking, yoga or swimming. Your body will tell you if you're overdoing it, so learn to listen and find the right balance of movement and rest that suits you.

The social side to eating
Eating is about so much more than just the nutritional value though. It's a social, connective experience that can make us feel happy. So many global traditions have food at their core. For many people, Christmas means the whole family eating together, sharing roast turkey with all the trimmings, for example. Certain foods become linked in our conscious with happiness, and that comes from the experience itself as much as the specific foods.

Sharing meals with people has a lot of benefits. There is the celebratory aspect, bringing friends and family together to enjoy a meal for a special occasion, which can boost your mood. However, it's also important in other ways. The Mental Heath Foundation says that sharing meals with others regularly "has many psychological, social and biological benefits. They give us a sense of rhythm and regularity in our lives, a chance to reflect on the day and feel connected to others." Where possible, sitting down to eat one meal a day with others can be hugely beneficial to your mental wellbeing.

Different foods can also make us feel happy – and it's not always the foods that are nutritionally good for us. We've all experienced that blissy, relaxed sensation when savouring a bar of our favourite chocolate, or a feeling of contentment when ordering a takeaway for a cosy night in. These foods trigger the release of certain hormones in the brain, which is why we want more of them.

Eating a good meal makes us feel happy through the release of dopamine – the feel-good hormone. In fact, one German study** suggests that we actually get two different dopamine hits from a meal. The first comes when we actually eat the food, which triggers the reward and sensory areas of the brain – this hit is higher with foods that we really enjoy eating, which makes us crave and want more. The second comes later, once the food hits the stomach, which is linked to higher cognitive functions. Two happy hormone hits for the price of one? Sounds great, doesn't it? However, as always, moderation is key. The study also found that the bigger the craving for a food (and hence the bigger release of the initial reward-based dopamine), the less of the second, cognition-boosting dopamine was released.

The message here is that most of the food we eat should be healthy and balanced, with a wide variety to ensure we get all those mood-boosting nutrients and that slow-released dopamine burst, ideally eaten with

LIVE YOURSELF HAPPY

others some of the time. But there's also a little room to enjoy foods that hit the sweet spot and give a more immediate burst of joy.

Adding in exercise

The other part of the lifestyle equation when it comes to mental wellbeing is exercise. There is so much evidence to show that exercise can have a huge impact on our mental health. It can help you to sleep better at night, which in itself can help to enhance your mood. It can help with stress, worry and anxiety, as well as all-important headspace and time doing something you love away from work and home life. Regular exercise can help prevent mental health conditions like depression, as well as lower the risk of some physical health conditions too. People who exercise regularly may also have higher self-esteem, more confidence and increased energy levels, which all help to boost your mood.

When you exercise, your body produces more endorphins – your happy hormones. This is why you often hear about the 'runner's high', but don't worry that you can only get this 'high' from running. Any form of aerobic exercise will have the same effect, as long as it's something you enjoy. This is the key part of any exercise routine – it has to be something that you do actually want to do. Forcing yourself into exercise that you find a chore isn't going to help your mental wellbeing. The point is to find something that makes you feel energised, happy and engaged. You're then more likely to want to do it, creating a productive and positive routine that you can stick to.

Exercise doesn't have to be running or going to the gym or lifting weights or playing a sport. Anything that gets you moving counts, so if you love to dance, do that! Or maybe try a long hike in the mountains, walk instead of drive to commute, jump on a trampoline, hula hoop or skip in the garden... there is no limit to what you can do. Part of the fun is trying something new and seeing what you like. For most adults, it's recommended to try and aim for about 150 minutes of moderate activity every week, or 75 minutes of vigorous activity. You don't have to do this all in one go – you could look to do three ten-minute exercise bursts each day, for five days a week, and you'd meet that minimum guideline.

You may find that you prefer to exercise alone, as that can give you time to yourself to relax and re-energise. Or you might prefer to exercise with a friend or group, which can boost your social connections – another aspect linked to happiness.

Mindful exercise

Not all exercise has to get your heart rate up. There are huge mental health benefits to including more mindful, relaxing exercise in your life. Yoga, for example, has been shown in numerous studies to help relieve stress, anxiety and depression when practised regularly. It also helps with boosting your mood, increasing your energy, improving flexibility and building strength – so it's an all-round winner! There is a style of yoga to suit everyone, so it's worth giving it a go, whether that's in a group environment, or at home following online tutorials. Yoga also focuses on the mind-body connection, teaching you to breathe with your movements and tune in to your body – this is something that many of us neglect, so even just one session a week can help you to switch off and feel energised.

Whatever exercise you enjoy can be done mindfully. The goal isn't always to go faster, or further, or lift heavier or burn lots of calories – you will reap far more benefits if you focus on what makes you feel good. On your next run, for example, hide the stats on your watch, and instead think about your surroundings. Combining the huge mental health benefits of being outside with exercise can really give you a lift.

The great thing is that no matter where you are in your lifestyle right now, even the smallest positive change to your diet and exercise can start to boost your happiness. You don't have to set huge goals; it can be as simple as a short walk after dinner each day or an extra vegetable on your normal dinner plate to start on the path to improved mental wellbeing.

> **" PEOPLE WHO EXERCISE REGULARLY MAY ALSO HAVE HIGHER SELF-ESTEEM, MORE CONFIDENCE AND INCREASED ENERGY "**

* Clapp M et al. Gut microbiota's effect on mental health: The gut-brain axis. Clin Pract. 2017 Sep 15
** Cell Press. "Your brain rewards you twice per meal: When you eat and when food reaches your stomach." ScienceDaily, ScienceDaily, 27 December 2018

Meditation & THE BRAIN

Training the brain to remain in the present moment can ease stress, reduce anxiety and even lower blood pressure. But how does it work?

WORDS LAURA MEARS

The English word 'meditation' comes from the Latin meditari, which means to think or to ponder. But the practice has its roots much further east than Rome. It originated in India as early as 4,000 years ago, before spreading eastwards to China and Japan, and westwards along the Silk Roads into Europe. Now, as brain scans begin to pinpoint the neurophysiology of meditative experiences, and research trials explore the effects meditation practices can have on our wellbeing, what began as a step on a spiritual path towards enlightenment is fast gaining a reputation as a panacea.

Neural rewiring for health and wellbeing

There are hundreds of different ways to practice meditation, but at their core, most use a form of focused awareness to calm and balance the mind. Though research is still in its early stages, trials are starting to reveal the difference that even a short meditation practice can make to health problems like depression, anxiety and insomnia.

It's important to note at this stage some of the challenges inherent in unpicking the effects of meditation on the mind. It is notoriously hard to design studies that truly measure subjective effects on mood and wellbeing, and due to the sheer number of different meditation practices, it's often difficult to compare the results from one trial to the next. The meditation experience of study participants can be variable, as can the length and duration of the practices they're asked to perform as part of each trial.

The absolute gold standard in medical research are randomised controlled trials. In these studies, participants are randomly separated into two groups: one receives the experimental treatment, while the other receives a different treatment or placebo as a 'control'. This enables researchers to really measure the difference that the experimental treatment makes. But designing a control for meditation trials is tricky.

When researchers at Johns Hopkins University trawled through more than 18,500 meditation research studies in 2014, they found only 47 that met their strict criteria for proper study design and control. But within those 47 high-quality research papers, there were some clear psychological benefits: an eight-week meditation practice showed to improve symptoms of anxiety, depression, stress and pain.

This pattern of improvement in mental health problems is mirrored elsewhere in the meditation literature. Separate studies have found that meditation helps to boost lifespan, improve quality of life, lift mood and decrease anxiety for people with cancer. It helps to prevent relapse in people experiencing repeated bouts of depression. And, it can help people to cope with the symptoms of menopause and irritable bowel syndrome.

Meditation also has positive effects on wellbeing in people without underlying »

MEDITATION AND THE BRAIN

"MEDITATION HELPS TO BOOST LIFESPAN, AND DECREASE ANXIETY"

LIVE YOURSELF HAPPY

MEDITATION AND THE BRAIN

LEARNING TO LET GO

Steve Harrison dedicated his life to the practice and teaching of yoga after a transformational experience with a yoga master. We asked him why learning to meditate is so hard, and what we can do to make it easier.

"I think for me the first thing to understand is that meditation is a state, rather than a practice. It's convenient to say 'I practice meditation', but it's not really the case. We can create an internal environment that is conducive to slip into a meditative state, but you can't actually do meditation because meditation is where doing ceases to happen."

WHY IS IT SO HARD TO LEARN TO GET INTO A MEDITATIVE STATE?

"In a modern world, it can be unrealistic to ask a mind to be able to focus. The obstacle that most people encounter almost straight away is their own bodies. Physical discomfort is, for a lot of people, a distraction from letting go into meditation. Sore knees, sore hips, backache… the body just keeps interfering. Focus techniques are an incredibly subtle device that require an immense amount of willpower. It can turn into a fight with ourselves to try to calm the mind when the body is not agreeing."

WHAT CAN WE DO TO MAKE IT EASIER?

"The ancients spent thousands of years devising ways to help people manoeuvre into a meditative state. It wasn't only the mind that was worked on. If you can do simple things to work with your body and your breathing, it will do a lot of work on the mind without the fight. But the biggest thing for me, and I think the least spoken about, is our own psychology. Most of us are incredibly identified with our thoughts and our sense of individuality. In order to not constantly be pulled back into a thought stream about ourselves, we need to have a genuine interest in finding a space or an experience that's beyond our usual constructs of who we think ourselves to be.

"Ask yourself, how would it be if I just let go of myself for a moment? We don't disappear as a result of slipping into meditation, we expand."

health problems. It seems to improve working memory, focused attention and emotional regulation. In one study, participants listened to either a guided meditation or a language lesson. Then they were challenged with disturbing images. Those who had meditated were much quicker to recover from the emotional hit.

A quiet space and a comfortable seat
So how does meditation change the way our minds work? Many other tools that help us with emotional control usually work on the parts of the brain involved in conscious, rational thought. But meditation practices work differently. Rather than actively trying to control our thinking, meditation techniques train us to draw our attention away from the parts of the brain involved in reasoning and judging, and towards the more ancient structures that are involved in awareness of the present moment.

The brain constantly monitors incoming signals from the outside world, passing them through a structure just above the brainstem called the thalamus. It works like a comms relay, taking in sensory signals and forwarding them on to other parts of the brain for processing. Filtering this stream of information is an active process; we constantly and consciously have to choose what to focus on.

Our focus decisions are complicated by an additional stream of information, the

MEDITATION AND THE BRAIN

> ❝ MEDITATION TECHNIQUES DRAW ATTENTION AWAY FROM REASONING AND JUDGING ❞

sensations from inside our bodies. These are detected by the insula, the part of the brain responsible for interoception, or internal self-awareness. It responds to feelings like pain, hunger and thirst, but also has a role in emotional awareness, and links in with other parts of the brain involved in attention.

Deciding what sensation to focus on falls to a wide circuit of connected brain regions called the 'salience network'. It uses the anterior insula (the internal sensor), the anterior cingulate cortex (the attention allocator) and the amygdala (the fear centre), to listen in on external and internal sensations, before then working out where we should put our focus. And it changes when we meditate.

Meditation practices almost always begin by taking a comfortable seat in a quiet space. This helps to minimise the internal and external sensations fighting for our attention and, over time, starts to change the way the salience network operates.

During meditation, the thalamus remains active, still passing signals into the brain. But, with fewer distractions, the mind has room to focus in on sensations that often go unnoticed, like the feeling of the breath.

In experienced meditators, the connections in the internal-sensing insula change and strengthen, improving internal awareness, and grey matter in the attention-allocating anterior cingulate cortex increases, aiding focus and flexible thinking. Meanwhile, the prefrontal cortex, which makes decisions, weakens its connection to the fear-inducing amygdala. One study found that after just eight weeks of meditation, the amygdala even started to shrink in size.

On a whole-brain scale, imaging studies have discovered even more widespread changes. Measures of white matter thickness show that meditation can boost connections in the front of the brain, which contains areas involved in attention and emotional regulation. Simultaneously, regular meditation practice seems to prune connections towards the back of the brain, in areas that are involved in self-referencing and egocentric processing. »

TRY THIS AT HOME

Yoga teacher Steve Harrison shares a simple four-step meditation practice for beginners. This is an indirect method to do a lot of work on the mind without actually having to fight with the mind. Sit down, get comfortable, take some long, deep breaths, and create an environment inside in which the mind can actually start to focus.

BRING THE BODY INTO A COMFORTABLE SPACE

The one key is to be comfortable. Any form of physical movement or intuitive stretch can make sure that the body is as fluid as possible. Then ensure that the body is in the most conducive state to relax, without falling asleep. Sit on a chair, or in an armchair, but always ensure you have a straight spine in order to keep the brain-body connection alert.

SORT OUT YOUR BREATHING

If you're looking for the quickest way to create an equilibrium in your system, the breathing is the key. The state of the breathing reflects the state of the mind. If the breathing is agitated, the mind is agitated. If the breathing is calm, the mind will also become calm. Just gently start to control and deepen and steady the breathing in order to calm the mind without directly trying to control the mind.

FOCUS ON DEEP BREATHS

It's unrealistic to sit down and try to just watch your natural breath. Don't go too subtle too quickly – you will last seconds and then you'll be off. You'll have this constant ping-pong inside of returning to focus on your breath and then getting pulled back out again. So, deepen your breathing, because deep breathing is much easier to focus upon.

KEEP PRACTICING

You can slip into a meditative state by accident, but to slip into it at will requires lots of training. The mind that's not trained will generally be quite dissipated and unable to hold attention. But it's not necessary for the health benefits and the wellbeing to achieve the meditative state. Commit to regular, patient practice and just reach towards the point of meditation; there are a whole host of benefits that come with the journey.

MEDITATION AND THE BRAIN

Cutting out external interruptions and turning inwards during meditation rewires and reshapes the mind.

Focused attention in a wandering mind

Minimising distraction and internalising the mind is just one part of a meditation practice. The other major component is attention training. Many practices have a particular point of focus upon which to fix the attention; the breath, a word or maybe a sensation.

Depending on the focal point, different parts of the brain light up. Mantra meditations activate the auditory cortex. Moving meditations activate the motor cortex and cerebellum. And visual-focus meditations activate the visual cortex. But studies on blood flow in the brain have shown that, rather than direct the attention outside of the body, this kind of activity in a meditative state actually helps us to look inside.

Focusing on a single external sense, like sight, can activate the areas of the brain involved in internal sensing and, while this is happening, a part of the brain called the medial prefrontal cortex slows down.

The medial prefrontal cortex is part of the brain's 'default mode network', the circuits responsible for our sense of self. The network lights up when we daydream, when we think about others, when we ruminate on the past, and when we project into the future. It tends to become active when we withdraw from the world into a resting state, but meditation practice changes how it operates.

Inexperienced meditators often notice that the mind tends to wander during meditation: that's the default mode network activating. It's the brain's way of planning, processing and thinking about itself, and it can run away with us when our senses are internalised. But, with practise, people seem to become better

THE MEDITATING BRAIN

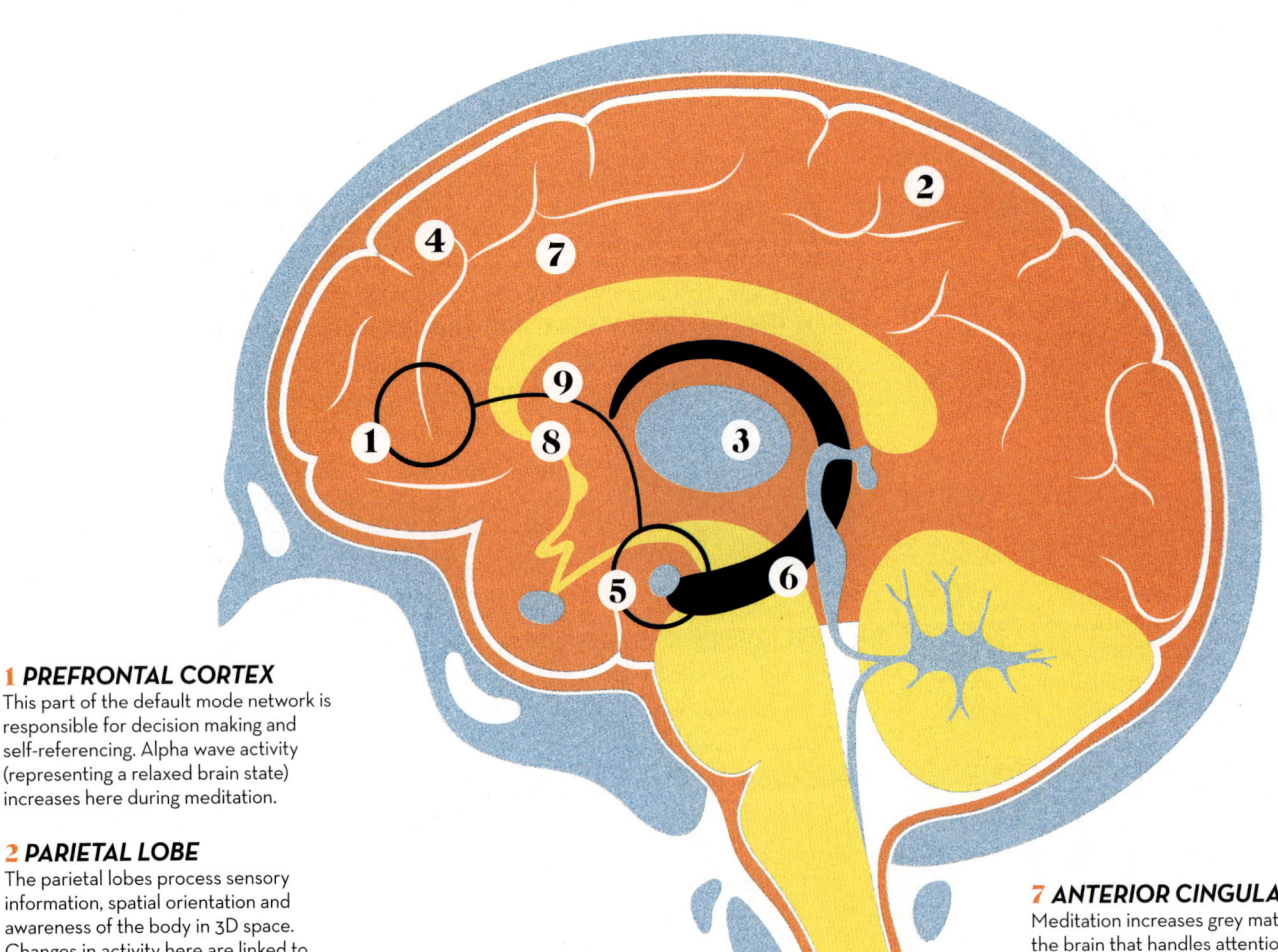

1 PREFRONTAL CORTEX
This part of the default mode network is responsible for decision making and self-referencing. Alpha wave activity (representing a relaxed brain state) increases here during meditation.

2 PARIETAL LOBE
The parietal lobes process sensory information, spatial orientation and awareness of the body in 3D space. Changes in activity here are linked to spiritual meditative experiences.

3 THALAMUS
The brain's sensory relay lights up during meditation as attention turns to specific sensations, like the feeling of the breath in the lungs.

4 FRONTAL LOBE
Activity in the large lobes at the front of the brain will increase as the meditator starts to consciously control the focus of their attention.

5 AMYGDALA
Activity in the brain's fear centre decreases. With prolonged meditation practice, this part of the brain may even shrink in size.

6 HIPPOCAMPUS
The part of the brain responsible for memory storage rewires in long-term meditators. The right hippocampus increases in size, affecting spatial memory and planning.

7 ANTERIOR CINGULATE CORTEX
Meditation increases grey matter in the part of the brain that handles attention allocation. This may aid focus and flexible thinking.

8 INSULA
Repeated meditation practice increases the connections inside the brain's internal sensation monitor, strengthening the brain's awareness of the body.

9 THOUGHT-FEAR CONNECTION
The link between the prefrontal cortex and the amygdala weakens with meditation practice, helping to stop fear and emotion interfering with attention and concentration

at noticing when the mind starts to wander, and can learn to gently bring it back into focus. And, with experience, the default mode network actually starts to slow down.

A study of the brains of experienced versus novice meditators at Yale University found that repeated meditation practice re-tunes the default mode network. But rather than switch off, the network rewires. The connections in the network that control self-referencing and emotion weaken, while those involved in awareness of the present moment get stronger. This could explain why, in a meditative state, we are able to witness sensations, noticing the breath, the body or the thoughts without trying to interfere.

Losing your self in the moment

The yogic scholar Patanjali described meditation more as a state of mind than an activity. The practices of removing distraction, internalising the thoughts and focusing the attention all serve to bring the mind to a place where it can enter an effortless meditative state. In this state, known in Sanskrit as dhyana, the sense of self dissolves, and the senses of space and time also fall away.

This type of experience is one of the most challenging to study because it is hard to conjure up on demand, but scans of Tibetan Buddhist meditators revealed that it might be associated with a decrease in activity in the parietal lobes. These brain regions handle the processing involved in picturing the body in 3D space, working out what's you and what isn't, and keeping track of time. Changes here seem to have the power to alter our perception of ourselves, not only during meditation, but also following other powerful out-of-body or loss-of-self experiences. In another study, which asked nuns to relive past spiritual experiences, the parietal lobes also showed shifting patterns of activity.

Body-mind connection and your physical health

Meditation has obvious effects on the mind, but can also induce changes to the body. Our psychology is powerfully linked to our physiology. Mental stress floods the body with a trio of fight or flight hormones: adrenaline, noradrenaline and cortisol. Their role is to prepare us to fight, freeze or flee. They raise the heart rate, quicken breathing and alter the metabolism.

Addressing feelings of stress using meditation can change the state of the body by transitioning the mind out of its 'fight or flight' mode and into its opposite 'rest and digest'. It flips off the sympathetic nervous system, which governs the stress response, and flips on the parasympathetic nervous system, thereby easing the strain placed on the heart and lungs.

Studies examining meditation in people with anxiety, anger and high blood pressure have found that meditation not only makes people feel better, but it also reduces physical markers of stress. Stress hormones drop, inflammation markers fall, heart rate lowers, breathing slows down, and blood pressure decreases. For some, a single meditation session was enough to see a positive change.

Molecular studies suggest that the effects of meditation go deep into our physiology. In a small study at Harvard University, scientists found that 15 minutes of meditation every day for eight weeks could change patterns of gene expression. Our cells each carry an entire copy of the human genome, but they only need to use a handful of genes at any one time. So, they turn sets of genes on and off depending on what's happening around them. A regular meditation practice flipped the switch on 172 genes linked to the body clock, sugar metabolism and inflammation.

Beginning your own practice

Meditation is an active area of research and debate in the scientific community, and there is still much work to be done to understand how it affects the brain and how best to use it to improve health and wellbeing. But one of the best ways to learn more about the mental

> **"MEDITATION MAKES PEOPLE FEEL BETTER, REDUCING PHYSICAL STRESS MARKERS"**

and physical impact of a regular practice is to experience it for yourself.

It can be difficult to know where to begin, but although there are hundreds of techniques, they can all lead to the same tranquil state. It's just a case of finding the methods that work for you. A good place to start is guided meditation. Allowing someone else to take you through your practice – whether at a class, or via an app, video or podcast – can help to keep you focused when your mind starts to wander. And you don't have to commit to a long session. Research suggests that just a short period of regular training is enough for noticeable effects. Be consistent, start small, and build slowly.

MODERN MEDITATION

Modern MEDITATION

Didn't think meditation was for you? You might think again once you've tried one of the many new ways to find your inner zen…

WORDS LOUISE PYNE

Meditation is nothing new. Humans have been paying attention to the breath and practising self-awareness for centuries, and for many years researchers have been exploring the benefits of meditation on both our physical wellbeing and our minds, with the body of scientific evidence steadily growing.

The list of benefits is pretty impressive. Slowing down racing thoughts has been shown to slash the risk of depression (or help treat it if you're already struggling with your mental health), by altering the release of mood-altering cytokines (inflammatory chemicals that are thought to lead to the development of chronic depression). It's also been shown to improve focus and attention, and help to beat insomnia.

"Meditation has been shown to reduce stress and anxiety, enhance self-awareness and increase the ability to self-regulate emotions. It helps you to get to know yourself, process what you are going through in life and puts some space between learned behaviours and knee jerk reactions," explains meditation expert and founder of Lunar Living, Kirsty Gallagher.

If traditional methods of meditation don't appeal, there are other meditation techniques that promise a chill fix. Here are some non-traditional ones you might want to try…

Walk your way to zen

Reconnecting with nature on a weekly basis helps to boost physical and mental wellbeing according to a recent study conducted by scientists at the University of Plymouth, and there's probably no better way to lower the stress scales than with a walking meditation. This involves bringing full presence and awareness into walking, something that many of us do all day every day without even thinking about it.

A separate study commissioned by the National Trust found that soaking up the sounds of nature relaxes us more than if we listen to a voiced meditation app, and results from tests showed that it reduced feelings of stress and anxiety by over a fifth. Connect with your senses on a mindful level »

> "RECONNECTING WITH NATURE ON A WEEKLY BASIS HELPS TO BOOST PHYSICAL AND MENTAL WELLBEING"

MODERN MEDITATION

MODERN MEDITATION

to experience all that new seasons have to give, from crunching leaves, crackling fires and the pitter patter of a rainy day.

"Begin by simply standing and bringing your awareness into your body, where you feel the weight, how you're standing on the earth, bring full awareness and presence into your body. Then begin to walk slowly and feel each step mindfully. Put your awareness fully and completely into how it feels to be walking; fully experience the act of walking," shares Kirsty. Every time you notice your mind wandering, stop, bring your attention back into your body and begin walking again. Try to be truly present in that moment in the act of walking.

Harness the power of crystals

Semi-precious stones and crystals have been used for thousands of years to cure ailments and support emotional wellbeing. During the first lockdown of 2020, there was a surge in Google searches for 'healing crystals'. Crystal enthusiasts claim that these powerful gemstones hold energetic and healing frequencies that can be a helpful aid to meditation.

"For example, rose quartz will help amplify love, self-love, healing of the heart and energies of compassion and acceptance. Citrine will help with abundance and happiness. Amethyst will help bring calm and relaxing vibes, and something like black tourmaline will

3 MEDITATION TIPS FOR NEWBIES

1. MAKE A SCHEDULE
Try to set a meditation goal for two weeks or a whole month. Even if you feel like you won't have time, once you see the benefits you're likely to want to find the time to practise. Allocating roughly the same time for your practice each day will help with consistency.

2. KEEP A JOURNAL
Scribble down how you feel before and after each session. Even jotting down a short sentence or two will help you to keep track of how the sessions are helping you.

3. SET AN INTENTION
Not to be confused with a goal, an intention is something you want to align with in your life such as a purpose or attitude you'd like to commit to. Before each practice, set a specific intention to help focus your mind and heart. It could be to 'release fear' or 'to practise being kinder to yourself and to others', anything that is connected to your values and life principles.

> "THESE GEMSTONES HOLD ENERGETIC AND HEALING FREQUENCIES THAT CAN BE A HELPFUL AID"

help you to feel grounded and protected," claims Kirsty. "As you meditate with your crystal, it will emit these vibrations to you so that you can more easily begin to tune in to these things in yourself."

Some people find crystals useful as they provide a 'touchstone' through a meditation practice to help focus your intentions. "So, you can program your chosen crystal with what you would like to bring more of into your life and each time you sit and meditate with your crystal it will bring you back to your intention," Kirsty adds.

> **"SOUND BATHS ALTER THETA AND DELTA BRAIN WAVES, WHICH TRIGGER HEALING AND RELAXATION"**

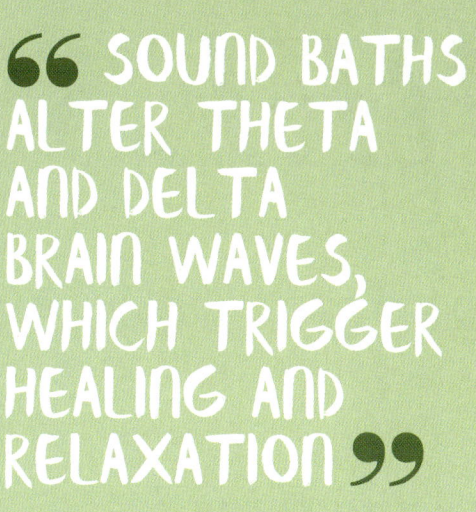

Boost sleep with beditation
With the pressure of work and family commitments, it can be a challenge to quieten your mind after a busy day so that you drift off to sleep. As many as 16 million of us suffer from poor sleep with a third confessing to insomnia according to one study by Aviva.

Sleep has a huge impact on long-term physical and mental wellbeing, and while how much we need per night varies from person to person, around seven to eight hours is the recommended amount.

A study published in *JAMA Internal Medicine* journal, which compared two groups of adults with sleeping troubles, found that practising a mindful meditation program was more effective at improving insomnia than a sleep education class that taught ways to improve sleep habits. And furthermore, if your goal is to improve sleep, practising meditation before hitting the hay (a technique called beditation) could possibly improve snoozing time more effectively than meditating during the day. "Beditation is the act of consciously releasing your day helping you to de-stress, relax and let go ready for a good night's sleep," explains Kirsty.

The great thing is that you can practise beditation from the comfort of your bed. "Close your eyes and take a few long, slow, deep breaths. Take a mental scan of your physical body and also how you feel energetically, mentally and emotionally. Notice anywhere that you feel tightness or as though you are gripping or holding on. This could be physical or emotional tension."

She goes on to add that with each long, slow, deep breath, simply let go.

"Feel as though you are processing and releasing your day ready for a restful sleep. Stay here for as long as you need to, simply exhaling and letting go until you feel a sense of becoming more relaxed and present."

Meditate to music
If sitting in silence doesn't do it, try a sound bath. This ancient therapy uses the sound of crystal singing bowls and chimes to ignite a relaxed, meditative state. Music makes us feel good, so it's no wonder that 88% of us turn to music when we need a boost.

Sound baths work by altering the theta and delta brain waves, which trigger healing and relaxation. All you have to do is lie back, get comfy and listen. Advocates maintain that the repetitive sounds and frequencies vibrate through your body creating a sense of peace.

Gaze at the moon
Celestial believers maintain that the lunar cycle affects our mood and energy levels, and we can tune in to its powers for guidance. "Usually we would use a new moon to meditate on what we want to create and bring into our lives and a full moon to do the work of releasing what we no longer need," believes Kirsty.

Living by lunar cycles is a centuries-old concept, but harnessing its purported mystical powers is something that we can bring into modern life, as Kirsty describes. "On the night of a new moon, make a list of your new moon intentions and what you would like to create in your life over the next lunar cycle. Then take a meditation where you visualise all of this coming easily and effortlessly to you. See yourself as though you already have all that you want and how that would feel. Sit in gratitude for all of your intentions coming true."

Once the full moon arrives, you can meditate under the moonlight. "Make a list of all that stands in your way and all you would like to let go of. Then lie on your back and begin to breathe slowly and deeply. With each deep exhale, feel as though you are gently breathing away anything that you no longer need. Feel yourself relax and surrender into the earth beneath you as you just let go with every breath," instructs Kirsty.

LET THE TREES
Treat You

From boosting mood to immunity, forest bathing is fantastic for improving our wellbeing. Grab your coat, get outside and enjoy the wonders of woodland

WORDS SARA NIVEN

We know fresh air is good for us and natural surroundings are an obvious choice for getting that, but while the coast can be calming, it is a well-established fact that wooded areas and forests are the most powerful places when it comes to restorative effects.

The idea of forest bathing, or Shinrin-yoku as it is known in Japan, where the idea first originated in the 1980s, has become increasingly popular and is supported by professionals in both medical and psychological fields.

"With over half the world's population now living in urban areas, we have become more removed from nature, but numerous studies show the mental health benefits of reconnecting, specifically by immersing yourself in a forest or woodland atmosphere," confirms Professor Stephen Palmer, founder director of both the International Centre for Ecopsychology and also the Centre for Stress Management. "Overall, forest bathing induces relaxation and enhances wellbeing while research has found specific reductions in levels of anxiety, depression, stress and even selfishness."

Come to your senses

To get the most from an experience and truly 'bathe', Professor Palmer explains that you should use all your senses – sight, smell, touch, hearing and, if safe to do so, taste. (The latter should only ever be undertaken with expert, professional guidance if tasting plants.)

To prevent distractions if walking with your friends and family, he advises staying a safe distance apart and avoiding conversation. Give each other plenty of space and it is best to turn your mobile phone off too. Then try these suggestions:

Walk slowly through the forest or wood, avoiding rushing. Listen to the sound of your footsteps. Take the opportunity to stop and look all around you. If you go at different times of the day, you will notice changes in the light. Your experience will also vary depending on the seasons.

On your next forest bathing session, when you stop, listen to the birdsong. Focus on a particular bird. Look up at the tree canopy.

On your following trip, you may wish to take a rug with you for this exercise. In the forest, assuming that it is safe to do so, find a flat area where you can lay down and gaze upwards. Look at the leaves. Notice the different shades of green. You may notice that you have started to relax. If so, slowly breathe in and out and taste the freshness of the air. Become aware of the natural wood fragrance found in forests.

On another occasion, softly touch a tree with your fingers, then with the palm of your hand. Reflect on what you notice. Smell the bark of the tree. Appreciate the time it has taken the tree to grow.

Forest bathing benefits

Forest bathing can boost your mood. It's been shown to help reduce negative emotions such as anger and fear, while increasing feelings of happiness and general wellbeing. Inje University in Seoul, South Korea, carried out a study of patients with major depressive disorder, treating some in a forest environment and others in hospital. Results showed that the four-week forest programme improved the patients' depressive symptoms and generated remission in patients taking medication for at least three months.

Incredibly, the physical benefits of forest bathing don't stop there. It can also improve your immune system and reduce levels of stress-related hormones such as cortisol and adrenaline. Western studies have tended to focus on the visual and, to a secondary extent, the auditory impact of forest environments. However, Shinrin-yoku also places an emphasis on smell. Dr Qing Li, a leading forest bathing expert, immunologist and author of *Into The Forest: How Trees Can Help You Find Health And Happiness*, reports that when people walk through a forest, they inhale organic compounds called phytoncides. These compounds actively boost our immune system and have even been studied for anti-cancer properties.

LET THE TREES TREAT YOU

Forest bathing has also been known to make us kinder to ourselves, and others. Recent research by Yasuhiro Kotera and Dean Fido reported an increase in self-compassion, common humanity and mindfulness in students who participated in a three-day Shinrin-yoku retreat in Fukushima.

Other field studies have confirmed that time spent in nature improves our connection with others. Research by the University of Illinois revealed that residents in city public housing who were surrounded by greenery felt a stronger bond with neighbours than tenants in buildings without trees, and they also felt safer and better adjusted to their environment. There was a reduced risk of street crime and lower levels of aggression between domestic partners. The residents with trees reported using "more constructive, less violent ways of dealing with conflicts."

So what are you waiting for? Head for the forest! Your body and mind will thank you.

BRING THE OUTDOORS IN

Even when indoors, you can still experience some of the benefits that forest bathing and nature provide. A study in the *Journal of Physiological Anthropology* shows that simply touching and smelling indoor plants can lower stress levels, while a US study of patients recovering after surgery found that those staying in rooms overlooking trees were able to leave hospital sooner than those with views of a brick wall. Berlin-based artist Libby Page specialises in large-scale paintings of trees, including forest scenes and canopies, and says clients often tell her they notice their mood improves after hanging her art.

"I choose to paint trees and woodland scenes because I personally find them very relaxing and am aware of research showing that even looking at pictures of them can be beneficial," she says. "I like to think my pictures bring some of the benefits of forest bathing into people's homes."

> **FOREST BATHING INDUCES RELAXATION AND ENHANCES WELLBEING**

EMBRACE THE *Blue*

Could spending time near water be the key to feeling healthier and happier?

EMBRACE THE BLUE

WORDS ALI HORSFALL

If you've ever fallen asleep to the sound of the sea or been brave enough to take an invigorating, wild skinny-dip, you can't deny the positive effects of being in and around water. The ancient Greeks soaked in mineral-rich thermal springs to help them feel better, and seaside trips were often prescribed by doctors during Victorian times. And it seems they were on to something, because now there's a body of science-led evidence to prove that water can indeed heal. Keen to learn more? Here's how to ride the wave of 'blue therapy'.

Join the blue gym
The great outdoors is a healthy place to relax and recharge, as many of us discovered when embracing the goodness of green spaces during the pandemic. But along with fields, forests and our favourite parks, natural water is an element of mother nature that offers similar wellbeing benefits. "The term 'blue space' is used to refer to our oceans, seas, rivers, lakes, ponds, streams and waterfalls – but can actually include all kinds of water, and research is increasingly showing how these watery spaces can help us physically and psychologically," explains Dr Catherine Kelly, geography academic and author of *Blue Spaces: How & Why Water Can Make You Feel Better* (£14.99 ($17.50), Welbeck).

The concept of spending time in blue space was introduced over a decade ago in the UK as an initiative by the Department of Health and Peninsula Medical School in Plymouth, and it's since been championed by wellness experts and water-lovers as a very valid way to feel good. The overarching idea is that coastal and natural water environments – dubbed the 'blue gym' – can be used specifically to increase physical »

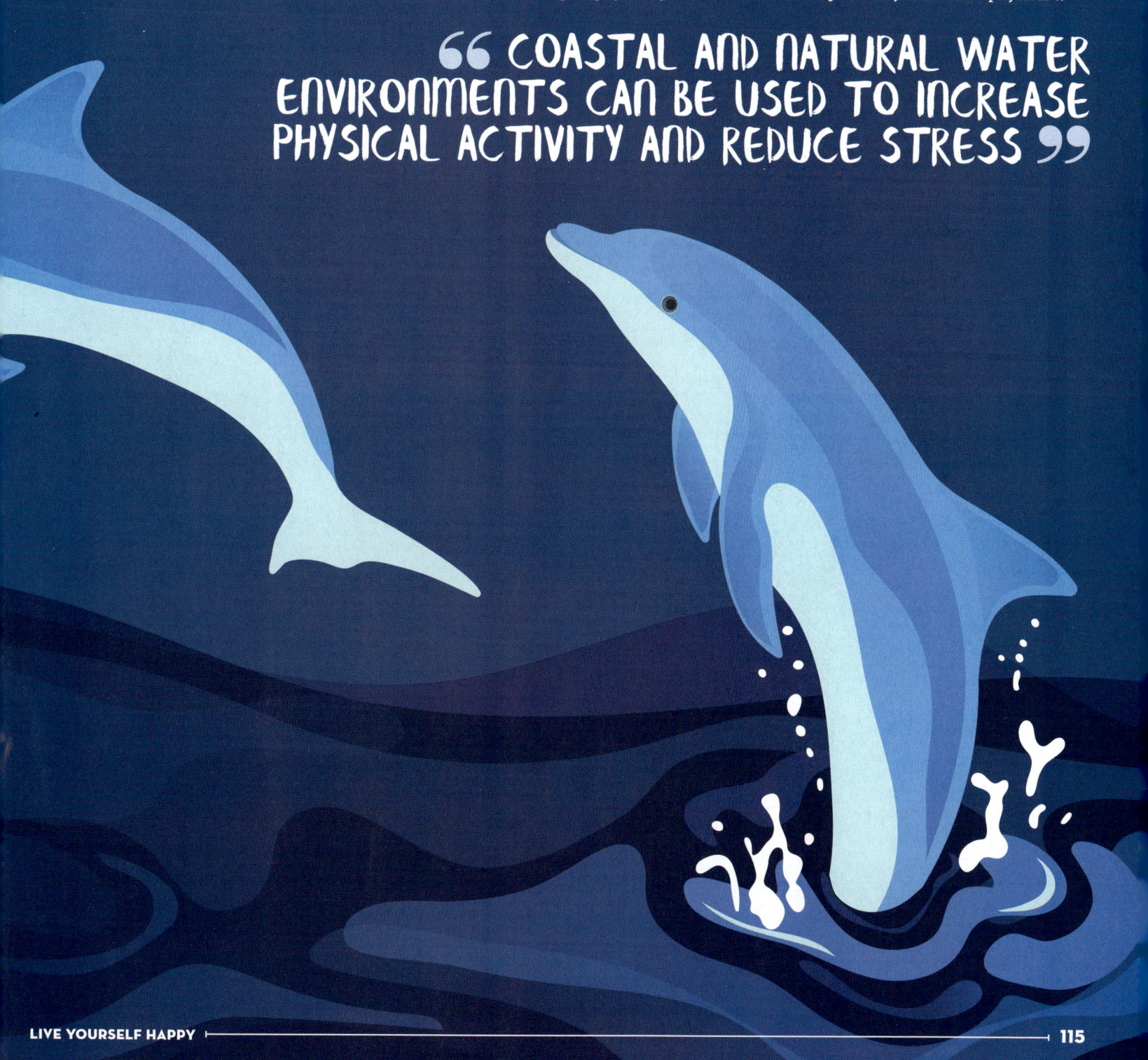

> ❝ COASTAL AND NATURAL WATER ENVIRONMENTS CAN BE USED TO INCREASE PHYSICAL ACTIVITY AND REDUCE STRESS ❞

EMBRACE THE BLUE

activity, reduce stress and build stronger communities. One study* found that living near blue spaces, visiting them, or even just enjoying a nice waterscape view, is associated with a lower risk of depression, anxiety and other mental health disorders, as well as encouraging relaxation.

A space to switch off
Ocean advocate Lizzi Larbalestier says she feels deeply attached to the Cornish coastline, where she lives and works as a blue health coach – helping others discover the wellbeing benefits of the sea (goingcoastal. blue). "I see people arrive anxious and stressed by the daily pressures of city life and the digital world. Stepping into blue space enables them to slow down, breathe and awaken their senses, connecting with a wider, more analogue world that has light, shade, colour and form," she says.

The environment proves to be the perfect antidote to time-pressured, device-driven lifestyles. "Blue space is a sensory landscape, meaning we engage all of our senses when we are in it," says Catherine Kelly. "We hear the sounds of the water ebbing and flowing, we notice the colours of the sea or stream, we can feel the sandy beach beneath our toes, smell the sea air or the wildflowers along a canal bank, and we can taste the salt on our skin after a dip in the ocean."

The outcome is positive. Busy minds will quieten without effort and it's possible to have tangible and tactile experiences that are not mediated by technology. "Water is medicine and in our fast-paced world, the sense of peace and presence it provides is undervalued and underutilised," says Lizzi. "You soon realise that we are part of an ecosystem, far from being disconnected and isolated, and that we each have a contribution to make."

Body benefits of blue
Research reveals that spending time by water also encourages us to be more active, whether that's surfing the waves or having a riverside stroll. "We then get all the physical benefits associated with exercise, such as improved cardiovascular health, combating osteoporosis and endorphin releases.

> "BEING NEXT TO A LARGE BODY OF NATURAL WATER INSPIRES A SENSE OF AWE. GAZING AT THE HORIZON GIVES A SENSE OF PERSPECTIVE ON DAILY LIFE"

EMBRACE THE BLUE

Plus, the happy hormones, serotonin and dopamine, rise when moving on, in or near water," says Catherine. Tempted to take a dip? Studies show that swimming in natural water may help with anxiety and depression, digestive issues and menopause symptoms. "Cold-water swimming stimulates the vagus nerve in the body, and this can induce an anti-inflammatory response, which researchers are linking to improved health," says Catherine. Visit outdoorswimmingsociety.com for tips on doing it safely.

Water for mental wellness
There's a biological reason why respite and reflection become possible in blue spaces. "Levels of the stress hormones adrenaline and cortisol in the body can drop, breathing regulates and the heart rate slows, so in essence we feel calmer and our mood improves," says Catherine. In this blue mind state, it's easier to practise mindfulness – water's meditative quality brings us into the present moment and allows us to press pause on our worries. "Being next to a large body of natural water inspires a sense of awe. Gazing at the horizon gives a sense of perspective on daily life and there's a feeling of being part of something bigger," says Catherine.

5 WAYS TO SOAK UP BLUE SPACE

Get the feel-good benefits of water with these easy ideas to work into your day

1. SWITCH UP YOUR WALKS
Blue space walking is a simple way you can connect with water. "Check an online map to find your nearest water sources such as a river, lake or canal, and factor them into your weekly walks," says Catherine.

2. SOOTHE WITH SOUNDS
Listening to water inspires calmness, focus and creativity. Even the smallest garden or balcony has room for a battery-powered water feature, or download an app that has sounds of the ocean. Try Naturespace (free on App Store and Google Play).

3. HAVE A RESTORATIVE BATH
A relaxing dunk in the tub will deliver benefits, says Catherine. Add healing minerals that are found in seawater.

4. TAKE AN ENERGISING SHOWER
As advocated by Wim Hof, aka The Ice Man, turn your shower to cold for an invigorating blast that will stimulate anti-inflammatory action in the body. "Start with 30 seconds for a few days, then build up to one minute, until you can handle two or three minutes of completely cold water," says Catherine.

5. ENJOY A WATER-BASED HOBBY
You don't have to sail, surf or swim to have fun around water. Try stand-up paddleboarding (SUP) – you can do this on lakes and canals. Sketch or paint a sea view, or take regular bike rides along a blue route.

Not near the sea? Get a city fix
Urbanites can still seek refuge in blue space. "In towns and cities, you can walk by a river or canal on the way to work, or find an outdoor fountain to sit by as you eat lunch," suggests Catherine. "If you deliberately notice the sight and sounds of moving water, you'll learn to tune out other stimuli. Focus on relaxing your breathing and enjoy a moment of peace." Many cities also have great outdoor lidos, which offer the 'fresh-air experience' while boosting social and physical wellbeing.

> **SWIMMING IN NATURAL WATER MAY HELP WITH ANXIETY AND DEPRESSION, AND MENOPAUSE SYMPTOMS**

*International Journal of Hygiene and Environmental Health

COULD COLOUR BE THE CURE?   LIVE YOURSELF HAPPY

COULD Colour BE THE CURE?

Discover how immersing yourself in the right tones can work wonders for your wellbeing

WORDS FAYE M. SMITH

Do you often have more confidence when wearing a certain shade, or feel more positive after walking in green spaces? It could be that colour is having a much bigger effect on your wellbeing then you realise.

"Colour is a quintessential part of life," says colour specialist Mark Wentworth (colourforlife.com). "Each colour creates a different physical and emotional response and, as we have evolved as a species, so has our understanding of the depths and intricacies of human emotion and behaviour."

But how we respond to the effects of certain hues, whether positively or negatively, can be very personal – there isn't a one-colour-fits-all when it comes to colour therapy. "On one level, colour is instinctual, and on another it connects us to our own personal memories and experiences," explains Wentworth. "Most people love something, such as sky blue, as it has an overall calming effect, maybe it reminds us of summer holidays and times of carefree daydreaming, and yet for some it's depressing, cold and detached." Hertfordshire University fashion psychologist Professor Karen Pine, working with Comfort UK, agrees: "We may love or hate the colour of our old school uniform, for example, depending on whether we have strong positive or negative memories of school."

With such personal responses to colour, there might be some trial and error when finding what's right for you, before you reap the benefits. "Be brave, experiment," says Wentworth. "Learn to understand your own colour language and how it reflects the highs and lows of your life story. Love your colours and watch your life transform." Here's how...

A wardrobe of personality

Whether you're dedicated to fashion or not, the colour of your clothing can have a significant impact on your mental health. You don't have to go head to toe – just a pop of colour will work, which is good news, as 34%* of women are scared to change the way they look. "Dressing for how you feel promotes an overall confidence and authenticity, which creates a positive approach from other people," »

> "DRESSING FOR HOW YOU FEEL PROMOTES CONFIDENCE"

says Wentworth. "If you have a goal, you can booby-trap your wardrobe with colour to attract what you want." He suggests the following...

YELLOW
is sunshine, brightness and fun. There'll never be a dull moment when you're wearing yellow.

PURPLE
says 'I am my own person and I'll stand out from the crowd'. Wearing it inspires creativity and commands respect.

BLUE
conveys trust and openness. We'd probably sit down and share our hopes and dreams with someone wearing blue, as blue overall tends to make us feel safe, whatever the shade.

GREEN
brings freshness and the impression that everything will happen in its own good time. When we wear green, we offer a level-headed approach to life.

BLACK
is sophistication and elegance – it adds style and class due to its ability to highlight everything else around it. It makes other colours appear bolder and stronger, and it conveys mystery.

Love a PATTERN?
You'll still benefit from the colours, but mixing them can dilute the effects, as intricate or repetitive detailing can pull focus.

Worried about wearing red?
Although a lot of people talk about feeling brave when wearing red, it can have negative connotations. "According to a study, men thought women were more interested in sex if they wore a red rather than a white T-shirt," says Professor Pine. "Evolutionary psychologists have shown that men ask women more intimate questions if they are wearing red. Women rate men who wear red as being more attractive."

Blondes really do have more fun
Feel more positive after a trip to the salon? You're not alone. A study by Nottingham Trent University and Clairol found that women who dyed their hair blonde had increased levels of confidence. It's thought that a strong and bold hair colour is similar to what we had as children, and therefore exudes a feeling of youthfulness. "Colouring your hair may seem like an art to most people, but there is actually a lot of science behind it," says Dr Mark Sergeant, who led

DID YOU KNOW?

Many banks use the colour blue in their logos, as do Facebook, LinkedIn and Twitter, because it helps companies seem trustworthy.

....

64% of Brits believe how they dress can make them feel better about themselves and boost their mood, says a study by Comfort UK.
Comfort UK's white paper, Long Live Clothes

....

A shade of pink called Baker-Miller has been used to reduce violence in hostile environments, due to the colour's calming properties.

> "ALTHOUGH A LOT OF PEOPLE TALK ABOUT FEELING BRAVE WHEN WEARING RED, IT CAN HAVE NEGATIVE CONNOTATIONS"

the research. "Not only were their confidence and mood levels elevated, but many reported feeling more attractive and sexually exciting."

Colour in the home
When it comes to the walls or decorations at home, following the trends can be a bad idea. "We should be wary of doing so when painting in our homes," says Professor Pine. "Our environment is an expression of our individuality – it needs to resonate with our emotions and provide a haven to return to. We will feel more at home in a colour scheme that chimes with our personality than one dictated by a trend." Don't have the same taste as your partner? "Choosing colours can be a minefield for couples so agree at the start that you may need to compromise," says expert Georgina Burnett, from **homeimprovementmonth.co.uk**. "If you like orange and he/she isn't keen, maybe this needs to be an accent colour in the room, against something more neutral like grey."

Boost your sex life
The colour of your bedroom walls and bedding could make a difference in how much sex you have each week, found a survey by littlewoods.com:

Purple – 3.49 times

Red – 3.18 times

Sky blue – 3.14 times

Pink – 3.02 times

Black – 2.99 times

Grey – 1.8 times

Green, beige and white are best avoided. "Dark green is a stop sign," says Georgina.

Kitchen overhaul
Had the same set of crockery for years? The colour of your plates could affect how you eat…

If you're caring for someone with health issues, avoid serving food on white plates. "They are the worst colour for hospitals," says professor of experimental psychology Dr Charles Spence. "With dementia or visual problems, there may not be enough of a contrast between the food and the white plate, so you want the food to stand out against a coloured plate."

Don't want to add extra spice? University of Valencia scientists found that those who ate from a white plate found food 13% more flavourful.

Researchers from the University of Oxford have discovered that if you eat from a red plate, you will eat less. "What you serve food on turns out to have more of an impact on our taste and flavour perception than any of us realise," says Dr Spence. "You end up eating a little bit less because red on a plate seems to trigger some sort of avoidance signal."

Flower power
The right colourful bouquet of blooms can help give a much-needed boost. "It's no accident that we buy people flowers to cheer them up or to express our love," says Professor Pine. "The attractive and fragrant colours produced by nature have an uplifting effect on our emotions." Not sure what to pick? "Yellow chrysanthemums are perfect for someone facing a new challenge," says floral designer Lara Sanjar, working with **funnyhowflowersdothat.co.uk**. "While purple anemones can help to keep you inspired for creative projects."

Immerse yourself outside
During the summer months, it's worth swapping the treadmill for walking outdoors in fields or woodlands. Experts at the University of Essex found that doing any exercise outside can boost your mood in just five minutes. "People have been soaking up the healing power of nature for centuries, but it is only in recent years that scientists have produced peer-reviewed evidence that there are measurable benefits to our bodies when we spend time among the trees," explains Beth Kempton, author of *Wabi Sabi: Japanese Wisdom for a Perfectly Imperfect Life* (Piatkus, £12.99). "These include increased mental wellness; boosted immune systems; and reduced stress levels, heart rate and blood pressure, which has led to the concept of 'shinrin-yoku' (forest bathing) being recognised as a kind of therapy."

* Mark Wentworth is working with Valspar's Love Your Colour Guarantee. It lets you change your mind about paint colour – if you don't love your first choice, Valspar will swap it completely free of charge.

WHY DECLUTTERING CAN BOOST YOUR WELLBEING

WHY *Decluttering* CAN BOOST YOUR WELLBEING

We explore the link between clutter and mental health, and how reordering your environment can help with everything from your stress levels to your relationships

WORDS JULIE BASSETT

Take a minute and look at the space around you right now. How does it make you feel? Is everything neat and ordered? Tidy and organised? Or are there piles of things that need to be put away? Clutter on the table, shelves filled to the brim and out-of-place items? Catch the thoughts and feelings running through your head when you observe your surroundings, whether that's calmness and happiness or an overwhelming feeling of worry and stress.

Our environment can change the way we feel, even if we're not completely aware of it. An untidy desk can make it hard to find the materials you need for the day's work, which can leave you feeling frustrated and unprepared. You might have an outfit planned for a special occasion, but when it comes to the time to wear it, you can't find what you're looking for or it's not clean, which creates panic. Are you always having to find your house keys, the remote control or that book you promised to give to a friend?

Clutter can build up in our lives without us realising it. We make plans for a big spring clean, a wardrobe sort-out or donating old toys, but when life is busy, we just don't find the time. However, living in an environment that's not ordered in the way that's right for you can have a huge impact on your mental health and wellbeing.

We don't mean creating a show home that dazzles in the art of minimalism and sparkles and shines on every surface. That's great if that's what makes you happy, but it's not for everyone. You want your living space to work in a way that makes your life a little easier and creates a safe space where you feel truly relaxed. To the outside eye, your home might seem tidy enough, but if you're fed up with the clutter and not being able to find what you need when you need it, it might be time for a change.

What is clutter?

What do we mean by 'clutter'? It's a selection of things that are placed in an untidy or disorganised way, things that are out of place or things that don't have a place. It's often those items that we don't quite know what to do with, stuff we've been given but don't really need, or objects we can't quite seem to get rid of because they might come in handy one day. Sometimes, items have a certain emotional attachment, even if they don't have an immediate purpose in our lives.

It might seem harmless enough to have a little clutter lying around, but if it's starting to take a toll on your mental health, then it needs to be dealt with. Clutter can increase your stress levels by acting as a constant reminder of things you need to sort and do, like a visual to-do list that never gets ticked off. It can also make it harder to focus and concentrate, or relax and unwind. Clutter in a shared home can also cause strain on relationships, particularly if there are arguments about finding things or different expectations of what constitutes clutter. We often judge »

> "CLUTTER CAN INCREASE YOUR STRESS LEVELS BY ACTING AS A CONSTANT REMINDER"

WHY DECLUTTERING CAN BOOST YOUR WELLBEING

HOW TO DECLUTTER SUSTAINABLY

One of the hardest parts of decluttering is figuring out what to do with the things you don't want. Sending lots of things to a landfill isn't environmentally friendly, and putting things in the bin can cause a lot of anxiety and guilt for many of us who are trying to live more sustainably. However, when you choose to declutter responsibly, this can make it a positive experience and boost your mental health. For example, if you have a lot of food that's in date but you'll never use it and it's getting in the way, why not take it to your local food bank? Clothes that are good as new that you won't wear can be sold or donated to a charity shop, helping to keep them out of a landfill and in circulation on the second-hand market. Try to be creative, too – something that doesn't work for you right now could be reused in another way or upcycled – turning something unloved into something loved can give you a real sense of purpose and fulfilment.

---

ourselves around clutter, too, worrying about the impression our home might give to others, or wondering why we can't get on top of it when it seems like an easy task on paper.

It's not that simple, though. When we're already getting pulled in so many different directions with work, family, exercise, socialising and household tasks, the thought of spending time dealing with clutter can feel draining. And the more it builds up, the more it starts to affect us. If you feel like your home isn't the relaxing space you need it to be, it's time to make a plan to get on top of the clutter bit by bit.

The opposite of clutter is order. It's not necessarily the same as thinking in terms of tidy and untidy, or neat and messy. The point is to find a system of order that works in your life, where you have the things you need, where you need them and when you need them. This can reduce strain, stress and worry, which in turn can improve your mental health.

How clutter can impact mental health
The physical impact of clutter is obvious. You can see the junk drawer starting to overflow, piles of old clothes gathering at the bottom of the wardrobe, broken toys that need repairing, or a garage packed with things that need clearing out. The mental impact can be less immediately obvious, and not everyone is affected in the same way. We all have a different tolerance for how much clutter we can take. However, there are some signs that clutter is beginning to affect your wellbeing.

Ideally, your home environment should be a place away from the stress of work, somewhere you feel relaxed and calm. This isn't always easy if you share a home with a flatmate, partner or children – more people in a space equals more items to manage. Having high levels of clutter can increase your stress levels; according to some studies, cortisol levels are higher in those who live in a cluttered environment.

Having clutter in your way can also make it harder to focus on tasks. Work duties can be more complex to complete if your desk is piled high with papers and books, and it can be difficult to keep on top of cleaning a space if there is a lot of clutter around. One study* found that 'clutter problems led to a significant decrease in satisfaction with life among older adults', while also looking at the link between procrastination and clutter across different generations. You're more likely to procrastinate on a job you need to do when there is clutter in the way – imagine you need to pay the bill that came through the other day but can't find the details when you need them, so the job gets delayed or forgotten.

If you live with a partner, you may find their clutter particularly hard to deal with, as it could be intruding into your space and make you feel like you have no control over your environment. Many parents also feel this way, as their children require more items that can end up cluttering surfaces over time, as well as toys everywhere. If your home makes you feel uncomfortable, to the point where you don't want to invite people over, this can also impact your friendships and other relationships, as well as increase your sense of judgement and shame.

There have also been links found between clutter and lack of sleep, bad eating habits and lower self-esteem. Clearly, getting a handle on clutter can improve many different areas in your life.

How does clutter build up?
It's easy to pass off clutter as a result of laziness – surely it's not that hard to just put something in its proper place? But this is very rarely the case. Even the most organised and tidy of people can end up with a cluttered environment.

It affects some people more than others, which can depend on our own personality type. For those with more perfectionist tendencies, clutter can feel distressing. There

> **WE ALL HAVE A DIFFERENT TOLERANCE FOR HOW MUCH CLUTTER WE CAN TAKE**

are those who find it difficult to sort and order, which makes it hard to get on top of clutter in the first place. For some, it can be impossible to focus on one task at a time, looking at the clutter as a whole and feeling overwhelmed, not knowing where to start.

It can also make a difference as to the kind of environment that you were brought up in. If you grew up in a home that was disordered and cluttered, you might either copy that in your own home in later life or rebel against it and seek strict order. If you try to maintain a neat and uncluttered home at all times, even a small amount of clutter can feel like it's hard to cope with.

Clutter builds up for a lot of different reasons. An overwhelming feeling, as we've mentioned, is often a big factor. It can feel like there's just too much to do - it's not just the act of deciding that something has to go, but it's finding a way of getting rid of it. This is why many of us start the process and sort through the clutter, but then end up with piles of things to sell, repair or donate in another location. The prospect of seeing decluttering through from start to finish can seem very daunting.

Sometimes, we keep things for other reasons. Items might have sentimental value, but no real place to live in our home. These might be things that have been given to us by relatives or handed down through the family. Maybe it's items that belonged to children who have left home, or older relatives who have passed away. This attachment can create conflict - we don't necessarily want or need the item, but we feel obliged to keep it or feel like it's just too hard to give it away.

We all keep things 'just in case' too. Those old clothes that no longer fit, but might one day; all those cables for long-disposed-of tech that may come in handy again; a huge assortment of obscure batteries and bulbs. We sometimes attach meaning to items too, that may help to define who we want to be and are part of the identity we want to create for ourselves. These could be things that we feel we 'should' have in our home, even if we don't need to, just to convey a certain impression. Or it might be something that we want to be part of our lifestyle, but never find time to engage with - a new hobby that we had an interest in starting, workout equipment that we purchased to get fit at home or the latest kitchen gadget.

The problem is that we live in a throwaway culture - there's always something new to buy that promises to solve an issue or change our lives. So we buy it, full of hope and promise, but it's forgotten about just as fast as something else comes along. Fast fashion, for example, makes it easy to keep on top of trends, but styles pass and the clothes just sit there, unworn and unloved. Often the quality of these cheaper items is low too, so they're harder to pass on or donate, cluttering up our homes with no real value.

Other items that we hang on to bring us a sense of comfort and joy, and that's a good thing. Decluttering isn't about ruthlessly getting rid of everything we own and living in a stark, possession-free home. It's about learning what we want and love in our homes, and what is causing us extra stress and anxiety. The answer isn't about having no clutter at all; it's about reorganising your items and giving those things you want to keep a »

DIGITAL CLUTTER

When we think of clutter, we usually think of physical belongings getting in the way. However, in this modern age, we also need to consider our digital clutter. If you have hundreds of unread emails, every text message you've ever sent, 30 versions of the same photo in your camera roll and a computer desktop full of downloaded files and random folders, this can also have an impact on your mental health. It can make it much harder to find things when you need to, which increases stress levels and anxiety. Try to organise emails as they come in - reply straight away, flag up for a future response, store in a labelled folder to refer back to, or delete any that are irrelevant. Archive chat conversations that haven't been active in more than six months, and do a social media audit to remove yourself from groups that you don't engage in. It can be quite a mammoth task at first, but you will find it easier to put systems in place for a fresh start once you've decluttered.

proper place in your environment, finding that important balance between clutter and comfort. Some people will want to display lots of items that are important to them; others will want a more minimalist finish.

Benefits of decluttering

Deciding that you need to get on top of your clutter is the first step. Acknowledging that something needs to be done and that it's having an impact on your mental health is a powerful motivator in itself. The aim is to create a sense of pride in your home, where everything is where you want it to be, where you feel comfortable and safe, and where you are happy to invite friends or family to share in your environment.

There are many benefits to decluttering your home. The act of sorting, organising and getting rid of items can help you to feel a sense of real achievement and confidence in your ability to create an environment that suits you. As you start to sort out one area, you will feel a boost to help you carry on to other areas. And in time, you will be less likely to introduce new clutter in the future.

It can also help to reduce your stress levels and anxiety, giving you back a safe and controlled space where you can relax, away from other life stressors. You may also find that you focus better around the home and are able to complete tasks more easily. Cooking, for example, is a lot more enjoyable if you can find all the equipment and ingredients you need with no effort. You may find that you enjoy the process of getting dressed in the morning more with a curated and tidy wardrobe to look through, boosting self-esteem.

Decluttering can also improve your energy levels, removing unnecessary obstacles in your daily life. When you know where things are, you can save time. Plus, you don't have to use your brain power to think and remember how to find something, freeing up some decision-making capacity for other things. It can improve your relationships with the other people in your home, as long as the decluttering process is worked on together to find a happy balance that suits everyone.

How to remove clutter

Getting started with decluttering can be hard, but there are some things you can do to make it less imposing. It's important to understand that you're not going to be able to do it overnight. It takes time to build up clutter – over many years in most cases – so it's not going to be solved straight away.

Start by thinking about where you need to start. Which area of your home causes you the most conflict? For some people, the entrance to the home sets the scene. If you feel stressed as soon as you walk in the door, maybe your hallway is your starting point. Or if you're struggling to relax and sleep, it could be that decluttering your bedroom and creating a calm environment in there will improve your sleep, restore your energy and give you the motivation to continue decluttering throughout your home. What will have the biggest impact on your mental health right now?

Also, think about your goals – what are you hoping to achieve? Do you want to create a system where everything has its place, to save you time and energy in your daily life? Or do you want to free up some space to open up your home and make it easier to clean and keep tidy? Or maybe you feel that certain items are reminders of a past you're trying to move on from and want a fresh start? Whatever your motivations, it's important to have a clear goal to drive you through the process.

Once you have a starting point and a goal, you can begin decluttering. Set yourself an amount of time – it's easy to get carried away, but you don't want this to take over your life. You might set aside a day at the weekend for bigger tasks, or try a mini 15-minute job every evening. Breaking the overall task down into smaller chunks makes it more achievable and can stop it from becoming quite so overwhelming. Don't be afraid to take a break from it too, especially if it's starting to create more stress.

Think about what items you really want to keep and that you need to find a home for. For everything else, decide whether it has to be thrown away, repaired, sold or donated, and keep these in different piles. You can then tackle each pile one at a time. You may need to plan a trip to a local landfill site, list items on a local Facebook marketplace or free sharing site, or pop into your local charity shop. This process can be quite cathartic; you are physically letting go of things that have caused you stress, but if you can donate items to help others too, then this can give you a sense of satisfaction. It makes it easier to give items away if you know that they are going to a good place to help someone else.

WHEN TO ASK FOR HELP

There are times when clutter builds up to an unsustainable level and you feel that you're unable to get on top of it. This is the time to get help from a professional, who can help you to get to the bottom of why you have clutter and what is stopping you from dealing with it. This may be treated with a form of cognitive behavioural therapy (CBT), which can help you to explore your thoughts, feelings and actions around clutter. It can also help you to talk through things like an emotional attachment to items, guilt around clearing things out, or any stress and anxiety that might be holding you back.

For some people, however, clutter is a by-product of another issue or disorder. Hoarding disorder is not the same thing as having a lot of clutter. It is a mental health condition where a person acquires an excessive number of things, with no space to store them and an inability to get rid of them. Some people with hoarding disorder are not aware that they have a problem and feel unaffected by the clutter. Others, however, find it too overwhelming to deal with and may feel a lot of shame and guilt, while being unable to clear the clutter themselves. Often it is a family member or friend who notices the signs of a hoarding disorder and tries to help.

Hoarding disorder becomes a problem when the level of clutter is significant enough to interfere with everyday life or is causing a lot of distress. It's not known what causes hoarding disorder, but it can be triggered by stressful life events, having a family history of hoarding, having had a lack of possessions growing up, or never having learnt the skills to sort and order items. Hoarding disorder can also be associated with other mental health conditions, such as severe depression, obsessive-compulsive disorder (OCD), attention deficit hyperactivity disorder (ADHD) or psychotic disorders.

> **" IT TAKES TIME TO BUILD UP CLUTTER, OVER MANY YEARS IN MOST CASES, SO IT'S NOT GOING TO BE SOLVED STRAIGHT AWAY "**

When you have decluttered, spend some time organising the space so that it works for you. Think about the objects you often need to have to hand and ensure they are placed in the most accessible, easy-to-locate places, and don't be afraid to display those things that mean something to you. If you've decided to keep an item, it has a purpose, whether that's because it's useful or because it brings you joy in another way.

Every time you finish a space, take the time to reflect on the process and how you feel. Do you find the space more inviting now? Do you want to spend more time in it? Do you feel calmer and happier? Hold on to those feelings, as this will help you to reduce your clutter going forward.

Moving forward with a new mindset

Once you've completed your initial declutter, the challenge is in maintaining it going forward and not allowing a state of clutter to build up again. This will mean changing your mindset and scheduling regular check-ins with yourself to ensure that your environment remains the way you need it to be.

You may find it helpful to routinely check areas for clutter. Knowing what we do about the link between clutter and mental health, a quick declutter from time to time is an act of self-care, proactively dealing with a known stressor before it becomes too much to handle.

You may also find it helpful to set some rules for yourself around what you bring into your home in the future. Try to practise a more mindful approach to purchasing. When you want to buy a new item, take a moment to consider where it will go, whether it fits in with your style, whether you really need it and if you already have something similar. It can be helpful to set yourself a 24-hour cooling-off period where you walk away, or log off if you're online, to consider the purchase, then if you still want it the next day, you can go back for it. This helps to cut down on impulsive spending, which can result in new clutter and ensures that you only buy things that you really love or need.

You may have some lapses in your journey. If you feel yourself getting stressed or overwhelmed again by clutter, remember that you have been through this process before and focus on the improvements that you felt in your mental health when you were on top of things. This can be enough to motivate you to get back on track.

By changing your mindset towards clutter and the items in your home, you are showing respect for your environment and for your own mental health, which makes decluttering an empowering choice for your wellbeing.

*Ferrari, J.R., Roster, C.A. Delaying Disposing: Examining the Relationship between Procrastination and Clutter across Generations. 2018

BREAK UP WITH SOCIAL MEDIA

BREAK UP WITH SOCIAL *media*

Step away from the Likes, the intrusive algorithms and the life comparisons, and discover the benefits of disconnecting from your digital life

WORDS JULIE BASSETT

February 2020 marked 16 years since Facebook was launched. Originally called TheFacebook, the service was designed to be used by Mark Zuckerberg and his fellow Harvard students. It then expanded to other colleges and universities, and eventually, in 2006, to everyone over the age of 13 with an email address. Today, there are around 2.5 billion monthly active users. Nearly 1.7 billion people log in to Facebook on a daily basis, and there's a good chance that you're one of them. Add to that Instagram and WhatsApp (also members of the Facebook family) and you're giving over a lot of your time to the hugely influential conglomerate.

There are many reasons why you may use social media: to catch up with friends, to read news from your favourite brands, to send messages, to interact with common interest groups or to keep up to date with events in your local area. These are all perfectly good reasons to use social media, but how often do you pick up your phone with no real intention and scroll mindlessly through your news feed out of habit? These social networks keep you coming back for more. The 'reward' system of a Like gives value to the content you post, which in turn feeds an in-built desire to put out more posts and garner more Likes.

And yet, for all its benefits, there is a darker side to social media, one that can have a significant impact on our mental health and wellbeing. The question is: do the positives outweigh the negatives? Is it time to take a step back from social media and find out?

One of the biggest problems with social media is that it can overwhelm us – do we really need so much information available at our fingertips all the time? According to the website NetAddiction.com, information overload is described as 'when you are trying to deal with more information than you are able to process to make sensible decisions'. This is in no way helped by Facebook and Instagram's algorithms, which detect your browsing habits and 'helpfully' suggest other things you might like to see. Read one article on a subject you want to know about, and within minutes you'll be bombarded with suggestions of related pages, products and articles. It can be mentally exhausting trying to process all these different options and tangents, to the point where you find yourself unsure of what to do next, what to buy and even how to think and respond. This 'social media fatigue' is leading to more and more of us opting to take a break from these networks.

A US survey from 2018 found that 42% of Facebook users had taken a break from checking Facebook for at least a few weeks or more, and a quarter had deleted the app from their phone. And in the UK, data showed a slight decrease in the number of UK residents who used Facebook between November 2019 and December 2019.

There are further negatives to our constant social media interaction. For a start, our online profiles aren't truly reflective of our real selves. We tend to curate the information we post and only present the version of ourselves that we want people to see. This can be quite isolating; of our many hundreds of online friends or people we follow, few of them know us intimately in a way that we can connect with them and share our

> **"RECLAIM THE TIME TO DO SOMETHING FOR YOURSELF"**

128

LIVE YOURSELF HAPPY

BREAK UP WITH SOCIAL MEDIA

SLIM YOUR SOCIAL ACCOUNTS

Not quite ready to break up with social media completely? There are ways you can gently step away while also keeping a digital anchor. It's important to remember that you are in control of your social media; you can curate your own feed.

Facebook, for example, has lots of controls. Set up a Close Friends list and opt for any of your updates to only be shared with those contacts. Similarly, set up a Restricted list, where you can pop all those colleagues and family members you feel obliged to befriend, but don't want to engage with. Next, do a good cull of your Friends list so you're only connected to people you really want to hear from. You can also opt to Unfollow (but remain friends with) people. 'Unlike' the Pages you're no longer interested in, and leave all the Groups you don't participate in. All this will seriously slim down your news feed and can help to make it feel less overwhelming.

Similarly, on Instagram you can create a Close Friends list. If following an account makes you feel bad, stop following it. You are under no obligation to do anything on social media – only follow accounts that add something to your day, and that you enjoy seeing content from.

thoughts and worries. We're more connected than ever digitally, and yet far more disconnected personally.

And then there's the problem of comparison. It can be much harder to feel content and happy in your own life when you're presented with picture-perfect daily insights into the lives of other people, who always seem to be richer, happier, thinner and so on. Despite being hyper-aware of how much we want to control our own online appearance, it's easy to forget that everyone is doing the same, and what we're comparing ourselves to is just someone else's presentation of how they want to be seen.

If you do make that conscious decision to break away from social media, then what can you expect? Well, at first, a kind of loss; a worry that you're missing out on something (FOMO!), the fear that you won't get invited to events, or might miss out on the latest work gossip. It will take a little time to build personal connections back up outside of social media, but the benefits of leaving social media behind will surely compensate.

For a start, it frees up time. Rather than mindlessly scrolling apps on your phone, why not reclaim the time to do something for yourself? Read a book, go for a run, hit the gym, paint a picture... all those things you have probably said you don't have time for, despite spending an hour or more a day on Facebook. These things will lift your spirits and nurture your soul. Make actual real-life dates to see friends and catch up over a good meal. Phone people and have a chat, write long letters, visit family – it can be refreshing to step away from digital communication and build strong, personal connections instead. Having strong relationships and friendships can help ease the symptoms of stress, depression and anxiety.

When you're on social media, you spend a lot of time thinking about the lives of other people, whether you know them or not, which can inflame negative self-talk. By stepping away from social media, you can return focus to your own life. It gives you a chance to think about your priorities and to focus on your goals.

Of course, there may be genuine reasons why you can't or don't want to give up social media completely. You can still take a step back and reap some of the benefits. For a start, delete the apps from your phone so your feeds are more than just a tap away. Track the time you spend on social media and set a personal goal to reduce your usage.

Turn off your notifications so you don't have the constant update alerts, and set aside some days that are free from all social media.

Give it a go and see how it feels – there's a real world out there, waiting for you to rediscover it. ∎

LIVE YOURSELF HAPPY   129

Live Yourself Happy

ACHIEVE TRUE HAPPINESS AND FEEL MORE FULFILLED

Future PLC Quay House, The Ambury, Bath, BA1 1UA

Editorial
Group Editor **Sarah Bankes**
Art Editor **Madelene King**
Head of Art & Design **Greg Whitaker**
Editorial Director **Jon White**
Managing Director **Grainne McKenna**

Contributors
Sarah Bankes, Julie Bassett, Agata Blaszczak-Boxe, Clare Bowie, Claire Cantor, Eva Gizowska, Rose Goodman, Emma Green, Josephine Hall, Ailsa Harvey, Faith Hill, Ali Horsfall, Natalia Lubomirski, Laura Mears, Laurie Newman, Sara Niven, Louise Pyne, Jenny Rowe, Faye M Smith, Sharon Walker, Debra Waters, Julia Wills

Cover images
© Getty Images

Photography
All copyrights and trademarks are recognised and respected

Advertising
Media packs are available on request
Commercial Director **Clare Dove**

International
Head of Print Licensing **Rachel Shaw**
licensing@futurenet.com

Circulation
Head of Newstrade **Tim Mathers**

Production
Head of Production **Mark Constance**
Production Project Manager **Matthew Eglinton**
Advertising Production Manager **Joanne Crosby**
Digital Editions Controller **Jason Hudson**
Production Managers **Keely Miller, Nola Cokely, Vivienne Calvert, Fran Twentyman**

Printed in the UK
Distributed by Marketforce, 5 Churchill Place, Canary Wharf, London, E14 5HU www.marketforce.co.uk – For enquiries, please email: mfcommunications@futurenet.com

Live Yourself Happy (LBZ5624)
© 2023 Future Publishing Limited

Most of the content in this bookazine has previously appeared in Psychology Now.

We are committed to only using magazine paper which is derived from responsibly managed, certified forestry and chlorine-free manufacture. The paper in this bookazine was sourced and produced from sustainable managed forests, conforming to strict environmental and socioeconomic standards.

All contents © 2023 Future Publishing Limited or published under licence. All rights reserved. No part of this magazine may be used, stored, transmitted or reproduced in any way without the prior written permission of the publisher. Future Publishing Limited (company number 2008885) is registered in England and Wales. Registered office: Quay House, The Ambury, Bath BA1 1UA. All information contained in this publication is for information only and is, as far as we are aware, correct at the time of going to press. Future cannot accept any responsibility for errors or inaccuracies in such information. You are advised to contact manufacturers and retailers directly with regard to the price of products/services referred to in this publication. Apps and websites mentioned in this publication are not under our control. We are not responsible for their contents or any other changes or updates to them. This magazine is fully independent and not affiliated in any way with the companies mentioned herein.

FUTURE Connectors. Creators. Experience Makers.

Future plc is a public company quoted on the London Stock Exchange (symbol: FUTR)
www.futureplc.com

Chief executive **Jon Steinberg**
Non-executive chairman **Richard Huntingford**
Chief financial and strategy officer **Penny Ladkin-Brand**

Tel +44 (0)1225 442 244

Widely Recycled

ipso. For press freedom with responsibility